Richard Barber was born in Essex in 1941 and was educated at Marlborough College and Corpus Christi College, Cambridge. Formerly an editor in a London publishing house, he now works full-time as a free-lance writer. His first publication, *Arthur of Albion*, on which the present book is based, originated as a Trevelyan scholarship project. Author also of *Henry Plantagenet*, *Samuel Pepys Esq.*, *Dictionary of Fabulous Beasts* and *The Figure of Arthur*, he was awarded the Somerset Maugham award in 1970 for his book *The Knight and Chivalry*.

IN MEMORIAM

SO·THE·HEART·BE·RIGHT

Joanna Defrates

1945-2000

KING ARTHUR

In Legend and History

Richard Barber

Parts of this book were originally published under the title *Arthur of Albion* by Barrie & Rockliff with Pall Mall Press in 1961; reissued by Boydell Press in 1971.

Copyright © Richard Barber 1961, 1970, 1973

CARDINAL edition first published in 1973
by Sphere Books Ltd, 30/32 Gray's Inn Road,
London WC1X 8JL

This book is set in Intertype Lectura

Printed by Cox & Wyman Ltd, London,
Reading and Fakenham

ISBN 0 351 15269 5

CONTENTS

LIST OF ILLUSTRATIONS

Black and white plates

WHAT place is there within the bounds of the empire of Christendom to which the winged praise of Arthur the Briton has not extended? Who is there, I ask, who does not speak of Arthur the Briton, since he is but little less known to the peoples of Asia than to the Bretons, as we are informed by pilgrims who return from Eastern lands? The peoples of the East speak of him as do those of the West, though separated by the breadth of the whole earth. Egypt speaks of him, nor is the Bosphorus silent. Rome, queen of cities, sings his deeds, and his wars are known to her former rival, Carthage. Antioch, Armenia and Palestine celebrate his feats.

Alanus de Insulis, c.1170

I

The Unknown Commander

Did King Arthur really exist? Who was he? These are the first questions that most people interested in Arthur ask; and in order to understand his part in literature, we must know something about his place in history. First of all, we have to move a long way back in time from his period of greatest fame in the twelfth and thirteenth centuries, to the obscure times seven hundred years earlier just after the Romans had withdrawn from Britain. Historically, it is a very difficult period to study; there is so little evidence, either written or archaeological, that the best we can hope to do is to say approximately when Arthur lived and what he might have done to earn his fame.

In a sense, it is a riddle with no answers, or several. So in the pages that follow, three possible solutions are outlined, all of them contradictory to each other. Within a short space, it is impossible to sum up their relative merits, but I have tried to show how each one is arrived at. The first is the answer which has until recently been the most widely accepted; the second is favoured by students of Celtic literature, on which we depend for almost all our knowledge of Arthur; and the third is a theory which I have argued elsewhere in greater detail. But even though we know there can be no clear answer, the riddle is fascinating in itself.

Britain in the fifth century AD underwent one of the most protracted and radical periods of transition in its history. The order imposed by the Romans was already crumbling when the legions withdrew in about AD 410; already the towns were in decline under a crushing burden of taxation imposed by a complex bureaucracy, and

11

the magnates had moved to villas around them to avoid these taxes. The withdrawal of the troops led to a temporary increase in prosperity with the lifting of this fiscal burden. It seems that the troops may have returned in small numbers with a rather less complex administration between 417 and 427, but the pattern of post-Roman Britain was evolving regardless of their presence.

It is on this pattern that the argument for our first identity of Arthur is based. The unity which Roman government had imposed on the province of Britain disappeared, and instead there arose a number of small principalities. The magnates who ruled these little domains were soon involved in a political and military struggle for supremacy over each other. By 440 several kingdoms seem to have formed, consisting of a loose overlordship in civil and military matters. At this stage, the most important of these kings, Vortigern, whose name itself may mean 'high ruler', had to repel a new invasion by the old enemies of the inhabitants of the Romanised part of Britain, the Picts; and to this end he invited the Saxons to settle in large numbers within his territory, only to find that he had exchanged a minor problem for a major one. The Saxons soon rose against him, and were in effective control of the eastern half of the island by the last decade of the century.

It was not, however, a situation involving two sharply-divided racial camps, each with its own leader. In fact, neither side was in the least unified. The Saxons were grouped into warbands, each with its own chieftain; these might unite for a brief period, but would soon range off on their own to plunder and ravage. The settled population of eastern England, such as it was, must have remained largely British for two or three decades, owing no allegiance to Saxon lords, but merely being their almost defenceless prey, though central England was disputed territory, and at one point the Saxons in Cambridgeshire had to build earthworks against British raiders from the south. Similar earthworks were thrown up by the British in the west; and from this and other archaeological evidence (largely on the Saxon side) a general pattern emerges of Saxon incursions up the Thames Valley, along the East Coast, inland from their Fenland stronghold, and along the South Coast. Their general advance was checked about the third quarter of the fifth century by a British force led by Ambrosius Aurelianus, but their war-bands continued to make inroads into British territory.

Possibly in reaction to the unwieldy organisation by which Roman life was regulated in the towns, the Britons had become more and more pastoral during the century. This is reflected in their methods of defence: instead of relying on a retreat into the security of the walled towns, which the Saxons rarely captured, hill-forts were built or renewed, while the towns were neglected. Yet some rudimentary form of administration survived, and trade continued until the early sixth century. The culture of the Romans was gradually forgotten, though it would seem that some of the leading families still looked to Rome as the centre of civilisation.

Only the Christian Church remained as a centre of literary activity, and even here few writers were at hand to describe the events of these dark years. Communications were poor, information unreliable, and history was a subject almost in its infancy as far as Christian authors were concerned. The Church still retained something of the vision of an immediate Second Coming in which the primitive Christians had so ardently believed, and this attitude did not encourage an interest in secular affairs. So only moral diatribes – which sometimes happen to give the occasional episode from recent history – and documents needed for the Church's own records, particularly the dating of Easter, were produced. Only three such works, relating to the resistance to the invading Saxons from the British point of view, survive. Two are very much later; the first is almost contemporary. Gildas, a Welsh monk who probably lived in the south-west of Britain, composed his *De Excidio Britanniae* (*On the Destruction of Britain*), sometimes known as the *Liber Querolus* or Book of Complaints, about fifty years after the period in which we are interested. He is, however, less concerned with the recent past than with the present, and the larger part of his book is a virulent attack on his British contemporaries. In the course of this jeremiad, he mentions a number of prominent figures – but not Arthur. His brief introduction is a history of the fortunes of the British from the departure of the Romans up to the exploits of Ambrosius Aurelianus, and concludes:

... nowadays his offspring have in our times declined from the integrity of their ancestors. ... From that time onward now the citizens, now the enemy were victorious, so that the Lord might test in this people the Israel of today, whether it loves him or not; until the year of the siege of Mons Badonicus, almost the most recent and not the least slaughter of these gallows-birds, which also begins the forty-fourth year (as I know), with one month now elapsed; it is also that of my birth. But not even now are the cities of our country inhabited as before; deserted and dismantled, they still lie neglected, for though foreign wars are at an end, civil wars continue. The recollection of the desperate slaughter in the island and the unlooked-for help has remained fixed in the memory of those who witnessed both marvels and survived, and for this reason kings, public officials, private persons, priests and clergy all preserved their own rank. As they died, an age ignorant of that storm followed, acquainted only with the present calm; all the guiding influences of truth and justice have been shaken and overturned; so that no recollection, not even a trace of them is to be found in the aforesaid ranks, save among a few, few indeed, who because of the departure of that great multitude which rushes headlong to hell each day, are of so small a number that the venerable Mother Church does not observe them, her only true children, as they rest in her bosom.

This extract gives some idea of the problems with which we are faced in trying to extract history from Gildas' hysteria. He gives us one tangible fact, the date of Mons Badonicus, but presents it in such a way that it is impossible to be certain what he means. It seems most likely that the siege took place forty-four years before he wrote, that also being the year of his birth. Other writers, however, among them Bede, who must have used a text at least three hundred years older than any we possess, interpret it as forty-four years after the coming of the Saxons. Neither solution offers a definite method of fixing the date. If the first reading is correct, the calculation is as follows: we know from Welsh and Irish annals that Gildas probably died about 570, and wrote not later than about 547, probably c. 540. Thus the siege of Mons Badonicus is unlikely to have been earlier than 490 or later than 503. If Bede is correct, we have to fix his date for the arrival of the Saxons (which was probably a gradual process in reality, and not a single 'event'); this was probably about 445 and would give a date about 489.

We also learn from Gildas that this victory was followed by a period of peace, during which the Saxons appear to have turned from raiding to settlement. This would at least explain why the Britons went almost unmolested for forty years, and is borne out by the slender archaeological evidence for the period. Mons Badonicus was a watershed in British affairs; but Gildas entirely fails to tell us the name of the British leader in this battle. Who was he?

We have to move on another three hundred years before we find an answer. Nennius, like Gildas probably a Welsh monk, wrote his *History of the Britons* about the year 829, that is, three hundred years after the battle of Mons Badonicus. He was working under very different circumstances from Gildas; instead of a lone voice crying in the wilderness, he belonged to a cultured circle with contacts throughout Ireland and much of western Europe. The Court for which he seems to have produced his history was that of the successful dynasty founded by Merfyn Vrych, under whom the Welsh at last appeared to have some hope of regaining their lost lands. There was renewed interest in the past, because to the way of thinking of the men of that time the past reflected the future in various ways. Past victories foreshadowed future triumphs:

> ...the wind
> Of heaven wheels round and treads in his own steps,
> Year follows year, the tide returns again,
> Day follows day, all things have second birth.

So Nennius gathered such records of the past as he could find, without much order or system, as he himself admits in his Preface:

> I, Nennius, disciple of Elvodugus, have taken the trouble of writing down a few fragments which refute the stupidity of the British race (of which they are accused) because their learned men had no knowledge and had not written in books any record of that island of Britain. But I have heaped together all that I could find, both in Roman annals and in the chronicles of the Fathers of the Church, that is Jerome, Eusebius, Isidore and Prosper, and also the annals of the Irish and Saxons and from the tradition of our elders.

In Chapter 56, he gives the first and only historical account of Arthur's military career:

> In those days the Saxons increased in numbers and grew stronger in Britain.

15

But at Hengist's death. Octha his son went from the northern part of Britain to the kingdom of Kent and from him arose the kings of Kent.

Then Arthur fought against those men in those days with the kings of the Britons, but he was the leader of battles. The first battle was in the mouth of the river which is called Glein. The second and third and fourth and fifth on another river which is called Dubglas and is in the region Linnuis. The sixth battle on the river which is called Bassas. The seventh battle was in the forest of Celidon, that is Cat Coit Celidon. The eighth battle was at the fort of Guinnion, in which Arthur carried the image of the blessed Mary, ever-virgin, on his shoulders and the pagans were put to flight and there was a great slaughter of them by the grace of our Lord Jesus Christ and by the grace of blessed Mary the Virgin, his mother. The ninth battle was fought in the city of the Legion. He fought the tenth battle on the shore of the river called Tribruit. The eleventh battle was fought on the mountain called Agned. The twelfth battle was at Badon Hill, where nine hundred and sixty men perished at one charge of Arthur's and no-one killed them save he himself. And in all the battles he was victor. And they, when they were defeated in all the battles, sent for help to Germany, and their numbers were ceaselessly added to, and they brought kings from Germany to rule over those in Britain.

So the victor of Mons Badonicus was, if we are to believe Nennius, an experienced campaigner at the height of his career. His account agrees with Gildas in placing Mons Badonicus at the end of the series of battles, because Gildas tells us that a long period of peace followed. But everything else he says is entirely new; no other writer gives details of the other eleven battles, and when we come across them in later historians, we find that they are always relying on Nennius. So at first sight there is no way of checking his version, and we are perilously near to either having to believe or disbelieve him. Fortunately, there are a few straws in the wind. Remembering that Nennius was writing a very long while after the events he described – it is as though everything we know about Queen Elizabeth I was first written down in the 1920s, and that there was no earlier evidence that she had even existed – he must have got his information from somewhere, unless he had simply invented it. His preface gives us some clues, but the only one which seems to apply in the case of Arthur is 'the traditions of our elders'. Now, in the part of his History following the section on Arthur, Nennius seems to have used a collection of notes on the history of the north of England, and this seems to have been one part of this 'tradition'; but much of it must have been handed down by word of mouth, and the style of the account of Arthur's career is closer to that of Welsh poetry. This poetry, which was recited by highly-trained bards, was heroic and historical rather than lyrical; and there are two or three surviving poems which are very like Nennius' list of battles in form. There may have been such a poem about Arthur, which gave brief details of each encounter, as in the recital of Cadwallawn's battles:

> The camp of Cadwallawn the famous,
> on the uplands of Mount Digoll,
> seven months and seven battles each day.

> The camp of Cadwallawn on the Severn,
> and on the other side of the river Dygen,
> almost burning Meigen.

And so the list continues, through 'fourteen chief battles for fair Britain, and sixty encounters'.

If we accept that Nennius' account is accurate and derives either from a fragmentary written tradition or from oral poetry, we have only one major obstacle to overcome. Why did Gildas fail to give the name of Arthur as victor of Mons Badonicus? One theory for this is of great antiquity. Caradoc of Llancarfan, in his *Life of St Gildas,* written in the early twelfth century, mentions a feud between Arthur and Gildas, the latter having meanwhile become a saint of the Celtic Church. According to Caradoc, Arthur is said to have killed Gildas' brother, the king of Brittany, and Gildas makes Arthur do penance for his crime. However, such biographies of saints, though they often contain traditional material, are always concerned to glorify their subject as much as possible, usually on the principle that the greater the rank of the sinner who is forced to repent, the greater the glory of the saint. In any event, whichever interpretation of Gildas' dating we choose, there seems to have been a long interval between the battle of Mons Badonicus and the period at which Gildas wrote, so long that it is unlikely that the unknown commander of the British forces in that battle and the chronicler would have met at all.

A better answer can be found elsewhere. It does not lie in attempts to discover an oblique reference to Arthur, or a description of him under a nickname, in Gildas' work; for Gildas only uses such techniques after the identity of his target is firmly established. The solution is probably in Gildas' approach to his work. Throughout, he displays a nostalgia for a vanished golden age of Roman peace and justice, and he looks back to the Roman commanders as models of energy and courage. Nor does he ever venture to criticise Roman conduct of affairs. Against this, he proclaims on every page his contempt for all things British, and particularly for the rulers of the British. He attacks the entire nation for their slothfulness in battle, and contrasts them with his beloved Romans. The last part of the book, the so-called 'Epistle', opens with his bitterest attack: 'Britain has kings, but they are tyrants; judges, but they are impious men . . .', and continues by castigating the public and private vices of the five British kings best known to him. In this frame of mind, he is hardly likely to mitigate his attack by a reference to Arthur's success.

This would not preclude a chance mention, which we might rightly hope to find. The reason why there is not even this crumb of comfort appears in his Preface: he specifically declares that his object is 'to relate the deeds of a slothful and indolent race rather than the exploits of those who have been successful in the field'. This phrase could apply to Arthur or, equally well, to Ambrosius Aurelianus; it certainly accounts for the brevity of his remarks on Mons Badonicus. Furthermore, Gildas gives remarkably few personal names in any case. We can only conclude that there is nothing in Gildas which either supports or detracts from Nennius' assertion that Arthur was the victor of the battle in question.

If we accept for the moment that there is a basis of truth in Nennius' account and that this includes the identification of Arthur as victor of Mons Badonicus about the year 500, can we glean any more scraps of information from his rather muddled list? Arthur is called *dux bellorum*, which seems to imply some kind of formal appointment as war-leader, and in one variation of the text he is contrasted with the 'kings', as though he were not a king himself: 'although many were more noble than he, he was the leader . . .'.

Apparently he leads them on twelve victorious occasions. Attempts to identify the sites of the battles have created more heat than light. Most analyses have tried to claim Arthur as a local hero for a particular region. The favoured areas are the Welsh border, the East Coast, Wessex and the Scottish border, though Kent, Cornwall and Lincolnshire have also been brought in. At this distance in time, it is impossible to place any of the battles with certainty on the modern map. Our earliest records of place-names which give anything except the names of major towns date from the tenth and eleventh centuries, leaving at least four hundred years between the date of the battles and the first possible version of the same name in another source. Even in Nennius' day, they meant little to readers, since one manuscript attempts to provide a series of explanations as to the British names of the sites, which only confuse the issue. In the twelfth century, historians like Henry of Huntingdon had already abandoned the task of identifying them as hopeless. Modern writers, armed with the weapons of philology and texts which Henry of Huntingdon is unlikely to have known, have produced some apparently plausible arguments; but in almost every case, the text has to be carefully amended to bolster up a preconceived idea that Arthur 'belongs' to a particular part of Britain. The most level-headed analysis of the names is given by Professor Kenneth Jackson, who concludes that 'only two can be regarded as fairly certainly identifiable, namely *urbs Legionis* = Chester, and *silva Celidonis* = the famous Coedd Celyddon somewhere in Scotland. Another, *Linnuis* = Lindsey, is probable. The rest are all conjectural or unknown; though there is one very slight reason to suppose that *Tribruit* is in Scotland, and *Mons Badonis* is on historical grounds somewhere in the south'.

As Professor Jackson remarks, it looks very much as though all that Nennius knew about Arthur was that he had fought twelve battles, and that he put together his list from other Welsh sources. If for the moment we put aside the question of Mons Badonicus and the unknown commander, and concentrate on Arthur himself, we find that Nennius is not the earliest source to mention him. The early Welsh literary sources, which are very difficult to interpret and date, mention him a number of times; and there are a group of historical references as well, to which we shall return. The most important of these literary texts is *The Gododdin,* written in the north of Britain about 600. In this, it is said of one of the British warriors at the battle of Catraeth that, 'He glutted the black ravens [i.e. with the bodies of his enemies] although he was no Arthur.' If this remark is not a later addition, and does indeed date from the end of the sixth century, it shows that an Arthur enjoyed at least a local reputation at the period. This is borne out by the early legendary references to him which are discussed in the next chapter; while there is at best only the shadow of a shadow of history in them, they support the idea of Arthur as a vaguely heroic figure of more than human powers.

If we look again at Nennius' text in this light, there is a good deal of literature in it. The battles could all have been borrowed from other sources, as they present some fairly close parallels with the deeds of other heroes, and such items as the battle at the City of Legions which seems rather like an echo of the battle of Chester in 616, the vagueness of the 'battle in the forest of Celidon', and the rounding out of the battles to twelve by the repeated fights on the Dubglas, all confirm Professor Jackson's suggestion that the core of Nennius' account is no more than a tradition that he fought twelve battles. In this case, there is no reason why the battle of Mons Badonicus should not have been 'attributed' to him in the same way. Nennius had good political reasons for wanting to find a heroic figure in early British history as an example and inspiration to his contemporaries, who hoped to redeem the Britons' otherwise sorry record of defeats. If this is true, Nennius did not 'invent' Arthur so much as build him up. The question that then faces us is: What did Nennius find in Arthur that made him a potential Messiah figure? What was the starting point?

To answer this we have to look at some further historical evidence. Firstly, there are two entries in a work called *Annales Cambriae,* the Annals of Wales, an anonymous list of important dates in Welsh history, taken from monastic records. They were perhaps originally notes made on a calendar or chronological table for finding the date of Easter. This dates from the late eleventh century in its present form, and the two entries connected with Arthur are as follows:

Year 72. Battle of Badon, in which Arthur carried the cross of our Lord Jesus Christ on his shoulders three nights and days, and the Britons were victorious.

Year 93. The battle of Camlann, in which Arthur and Medraut fell, and many died in Britain and Ireland.

Year 72 can be placed in 516–8 with the aid of the rather obscure paragraph which explains the basis of year 1 of the table, though this introduces a major discrepancy with Gildas' dating. Although the second entry is derived from an independent tradition, there is no reason to suppose that the note about Badon derives from anywhere except Nennius. Much ingenuity has been expended in trying to show that this 'must' be an early record, but the extant manuscripts are not only closely associated with Nennius' work; the actual text is a garbled version of Nennius' embroidered account of the eighth battle at Guinnion. Early entries in such Easter tables are to be found in Irish sources, where they are brief in the extreme, and almost exclusively religious in nature – the death of a saint or bishop, the accession of a pope – and these two entries betray themselves as borrowings from a much more elaborate historical tradition. Whatever the source of the second entry, about Camlann, it was to be a fruitful basis for the embroideries of later romancers; here is the nucleus of the whole tragedy of Arthur, his relationship with Mordred and the 'last dim battle in the west' which are for us the great and moving moments in his story.

The second piece, or rather pieces, of historical evidence comes from Scottish-Irish sources. The earliest historical document referring to an Arthur is not Nennius, but the *Life of Columba*, written by Adomnan about AD 700, in which Arthur son of Aedan mac Gabrain, king of Dalriada, appears. He is a warrior, who meets an early death (within his father's lifetime, so that he never becomes king), fighting an obscure tribe called the Miathi. There are other early occurences of the name Arthur in Irish sources, also associated with the north of Britain.

21

This evidence can be interpreted in two ways. If we accept the traditional dating of Arthur to the end of the fifth century, these names could be a kind of reflection of his fame, just as boys in the early nineteenth century might be named after Nelson. If this is the case, it is arguable that Arthur was a north British hero – *vide* also *The Gododdin* – whose career was briefly outlined in the notes on northern history which Nennius used. To this, Nennius added the victory of Mons Badonicus, since it was a loose end which he wished to tie up. There is just a possibility, too, that Camlann can be identified with Birdoswald on the Roman wall, known in Welsh as Camboglanna. Without going into all the ramifications of the evidence – and there are a number of very small pointers which cumulatively reinforce the argument – it is fair to say that an increasing number of scholars favour the idea of a northern prince named Arthur who lived early in the sixth century, and to whom the battle of Mons Badonicus was later attributed.

I personally believe that we can take the argument a step further. The dating of Arthur to the end of the fifth century or early sixth century seems to me to depend largely on his identification as victor of Mons Badonicus. Once we reject this as a later invention by Nennius, there is no reason why we should not look elsewhere for him. There is a good case, which I have argued in detail in *The Figure of Arthur*, for accepting the Arthur of the *Life of Columba* as the original of the hero. He is early enough to have been the Arthur of *The Gododdin*, and, although his name is usually derived from the Latin Artorius, all the early mentions of it come from Irish sources. The kingdom of Dalriada was an Irish colony; the kingdom of Dyfed in south-west Wales, where there was an Arthur in the sixth or seventh century, was also Irish in origin: and there are two other Arthurs in Irish records. Against this, there are none in native Welsh tradition.

In this case, Nennius' account would be largely a fabrication from literary sources to suit the political needs of the moment. Starting with a tradition no more substantial than that Arthur had fought twelve battles, which he found in his northern history material, he virtually created a new image of the hero with which to encourage his contemporaries (a process which we shall meet again in Arthurian literature). He arbitrarily assigned to Arthur the victory at Mons Badonicus, and thus placed him in the years following Ambrosius Aurelianus. There is no evidence that this battle was of other than local importance unless we accept Nennius' account. Gildas recorded it because he lived in the same area, and it did seem to him to have been a major cause of the slackening of pressure from the Saxons. It is equally possible that the Saxon advance lost impetus simply because they had reached the natural barrier of the upland areas of the west and north. Again, it is a question of whether we accept Gildas and Nennius at face value, or attempt to set them in perspective, as part of a cultural situation. In the case of Gildas, we must allow for the narrowness of his horizon; in the case of Nennius, for the mood of the Welsh when he was writing. In neither case is there any suggestion that they are trying to write purely factual and unbiased accounts; history, for them, has its own purpose.

In contrast to these speculations – and for the moment they are no more than speculations – archaeology would seem to offer good hope for a more definite answer to the problem of Arthurian identity. But the nature of archaeological evidence for this period is such that it poses more problems than it solves. For any archaeological evidence is useless without a clear time-scale into which it can be fitted; and the historical time-scale simply does not exist for events in Britain between the end of the fourth century and the beginning of the seventh century. There are odds and ends of definite fact, there are general trends of culture; but the relationship between one and the other is loose and uncertain, because there are no fixed points of reference. Even apparently unequivocal evidence, an inscription or a grave-stone, becomes vague and difficult to use without some external means of arriving at the true context. So while archaeology can tell us a great deal about the kind of place that Britain was during this period, how Arthur might have lived, it cannot help us to resolve the central problem: who was Arthur and when did he live?

In this context, the association of Cadbury Castle with Arthur rests on a foundation so slight that it is scarcely worth serious consideration. The chain of inference runs as follows: Arthur was a commander in the south-west (which, as we have seen, is certainly questionable) – Cadbury is the only major fifth-century refortified earthwork in the area, with signs of substantial timber buildings and ramparts – such a place must belong to the most important military figure in the area – therefore it is probably Arthur's. Alas, the truth is that a much more likely but very much less attractive candidate would be one of Gildas' unsavoury petty tyrants. As for its identification a thousand years after the so-called 'Arthurian period' as Camelot, this carries no more weight than any other of the Arthurian place-names of the later Middle Ages. Camelot was invented by a French writer in the twelfth century, and probably derives from Pliny's mention of Colchester, the Roman *Camulodunum*, in his *Natural History*.

What then is the irreducible minimum of Arthurian fact? We can say only this: that Arthur was a hero of the Welsh, celebrated in their literature by the eighth century AD. Where he came from, who he was, and, apart from being a warrior, what he did, we do not know with any degree of certainty. We may think that we can discern a particular shadow behind the legend; but to take it for more than a shadow would be a grave mistake. On the other hand, whether he was the victor of Mons Badonicus, a north British chieftan or a prince of Dalriada, Arthur won a reputation in his lifetime that gave him a special place in the memory of the British people.

2

From Reality to Romance

If the historical Arthur is shadowy enough, the Arthur of early Welsh literature is scarcely more substantial. This is partly because we only possess fragments of early Welsh poetry, in which Arthur's appearances are tantalisingly brief, even as a purely poetic hero. So the process by which the first legends were woven around whatever historical nucleus there once was remains a puzzle.

As it is, the remnants of the work of the Welsh bards yield nothing more than hints at what may have been a considerable body of stories. Nennius, whose account of the twelve battles is the main source for the supposed historical Arthur, tells us something about the legendary Arthur in an appendix to the *History of the Britons* entitled *Mirabilia* or *Marvels*. Among these episodes there are two which connect Arthur with place-names. At Carn Cabal, Nennius tells us, in the region of Buelt (Breconshire), there is a stone bearing the footprints of Arthur's hound Cabal while he hunted the boar Troit. This story reappears in the twelfth-century collection of Welsh romances generally called *The Mabinogion* as one of the main incidents of the story of *Culhwch and Olwen*, where Arthur and his followers pursue the magical boar Twrch Troit; and this boar-hunt was certainly one of the earliest Arthurian stories.

Elsewhere in the *Marvels*, Nennius describes the grave of Arthur's son Amr or Anir. This tomb, in the region of Ercing (Herefordshire), may be measured as often as anyone cares to do it, but the result will never be the same twice running. Amr, so Nennius says, was slain by his father Arthur, an incident quite foreign to the usual idea of the latter. We tend to think of him exclusively as a paragon of chivalry; but in this we are deceived by the influence of later English and French writers, for this was never the view of the Welsh themselves. We shall find a similarly uncharacteristic tendency in the twelfth-century lives of the Welsh saints; for, just as the chivalric romances reflect the times in which they were written, so these Welsh legends in a cruder and less civilised vein attributed to Arthur the morals of their contemporaries. However, some of the incidents in which his character is blackened are due to a deliberate desire to contrast him unfavourably with some saint or other; and this attitude of saintly biographers does not necessarily represent the real contemporary opinion of Arthur.

Arthur's role in Welsh legend may vary from the ideal to the criminal, but the emphasis was usually on the favourable side. On two occasions he appears as the leader of a band of heroic warriors, a picture of him which was later to lead to his becoming the idle king, *le roi fainéant*, of the romances, who stayed at home in splendour while his knights underwent the hardships and adventures. In our first poem, he does play an active part, but the narrative soon switches to his knights' exploits. It is one of an early thirteenth-century collection of poems, the Black Book of Carmarthen; but it was probably written down in the early eleventh century, and may contain much older material. Arthur is speaking to a doorkeeper about his company of knights. Among them are many heroes who appear only fleetingly in Welsh literature, but two, Cai and Bedwyr (or Kay and Bedivere in Malory's spelling) are immediately familiar. Some of their feats are described by Arthurs including the slaying of the monster Palug's Cat, but the poem breaks off in mid-sentence.

The Book of Taliesin, a collection of about the year 1200, contains a poem entitled *The Spoils of Annwfn*, whose basis is much earlier oral tradition. It portrays Arthur as leader of an expedition to a Celtic otherworld, an earthly realm occupied by supernatural beings, full of strange and magical treasures. He sets out with enough warriors to fill his ship Pridwen seven times, apparently with the object of fetching a magic cauldron from this realm, and returns with only seven men. It is a very difficult text to interpret, and has been given both historical and mythological meanings; the last two stanzas still defy coherent translation. The idea of an expedition to fetch a magical cauldron recurs in *Culhwch and Olwen*, where the cauldron belongs to the High Steward of the King of Ireland. This romance is rather later than *The Spoils of Annwfn*, but it is reasonably complete and on a much larger scale. It dates from the early twelfth century, when, as we shall see, other nations than the Welsh were beginning to take an interest in Arthurian material, but its conception and contents are pure Welsh. The themes are drawn from the common stock of folk-tales and the plot concerns the wooing and winning of Olwen, a giant's daughter, by Culhwch, Arthur's nephew. To gain her hand, he has to carry out a series of seemingly impossible tasks. The names and exploits of the heroes come from earlier Welsh works, adapted as necessary. For instance, the hunting of the boar Troit, the main episode of the poem, has been given precise details in such a way as to make it possible for us even now to trace on a map the course followed by Arthur and his men in their pursuit across large areas of south-west Wales and the Severn estuary, which the story-teller must have known personally. This is one of the most attractive of the stories known as *The Mabinogion*; it has a strongly Celtic and epic flavour in the emphasis on heroes and heroic deeds, with little of the more sophisticated interest in the psychology of the French romances and their derivatives. Despite its relatively late date, it was written without foreign influence, for all the heroes named can be found in earlier Welsh works. Here the rich fantasy of the Celtic imagination is at its marvel-loving best, with a very different series of adventures from those usually associated with Arthurian stories. The world it portrays is less formal and logical than that of the knightly romances, more given to the mysterious and supernatural.

Another genre peculiar to Welsh literature yields further references to Arthur, but by its very nature sets more problems than it solves. This is the triad: a group of three connected people, incidents or things, perhaps used as an *aide-mémoire* by the bardic story-tellers, so that, having finished one story they could lead on without hesitation to the next. Unfortunately only these 'headlines' have been preserved, and they are rarely more than half a dozen lines in length. Hence we gather little more about the legendary figure of Arthur from them, although there is no shortage of triads that include him. Indeed, the traditional formula 'Three . . . of the Island of Britain' is replaced in some late triads from the thirteenth and fourteenth centuries by 'Three . . . of Arthur's Court', but this only reflects his increasing popularity as the years went by. Among the early triads, however, several characters whom we shall meet later in the romances make their first appearances. Two triads mention Guinevere, his wife; and one, indeed, tells of the three Guineveres, all perhaps wedded to him in turn. This story may have found a faint echo in 1191 when Arthur's supposed body was exhumed at Glastonbury, with that of Guinevere, *uxore sua secunda*, 'his second wife'. Again, in the great French prose romances called the Vulgate Cycle, we meet the true and false Guineveres who are confused with each other by Arthur as a result of magic worked by his enemy, Queen Morgan le Fay. Another triad connects Mordred with Guinevere for the first time: Mordred is said to have raided Arthur's Court in Cornwall in one of the *Three Unrestrained Ravagings*, dragged Guinevere from her chair and struck her. But it is not clear that Mordred fought *against* Arthur at Camlann as a result; all that we learn in another triad is that a blow 'struck upon Guinevere' by her sister Gwenhyfach resulted in 'the Action of the Battle of Camlann'.

Of the characters less intimately connected with Arthur himself, three are present in the triads. Tristram and Iseult appear, under the names of Drustan mab Tallwch and Essyllt. Tristram himself was probably an historical north British king with the Pictish name Drust, of the sixth century. Essyllt is not specifically connected with him, but appears in the same triad. Merchyon, better known to us as King Mark of Cornwall, Iseult's husband, is also mentioned here. Another hero of the later romances, Ywain, is here too, under the name Owein ap Urien; there is reason to believe that he too was an historical prince of northern origin of the sixth century, absorbed into literature in much the same way as Arthur. And Merlin appears for the first time, not in the triads, but in poems about a prophet called Myrddin, distantly linked with the historical figure of St Kentigern in the seventh century.

So the portrait of the legendary Arthur in Wales is even less clearly outlined than that of the historical Arthur, though we have strong evidence for a considerable body of stories centred about him. This is reinforced when we turn to the biographies of Welsh saints written in Latin in the eleventh and twelfth centuries. These, though usually of little literary or historical significance, contain several references to Arthur, including two or three actual incidents from his legendary career, though these may have been invented to suit the particular work in hand. They are, however, evidence of his popularity as a hero at about this time.

The first two stories are to be found in the *Life of St Cadoc*, written by one Llifris of Llancarfan about 1075. Arthur is here halfway between the leader of Welsh tradition and the ruler of later legend, though he is not very favourably regarded by the author. If he and his companions are called *heroes strenui*, valiant heroes, it is only on account of their physical prowess, and the general portrait is of a petty tyrant. He first appears playing dice on a hilltop with Kay and Bedivere, and attempts to ravish a girl eloping with her lover, instead of rescuing them from their pursuers, until dissuaded by his companions; he then successfully defends the fugitives. He later reappears in a quarrel over blood-money for three men of his who have been killed, and is only cured of his obstinate refusal to accept anything except cattle of a certain colour by a miracle worked by St Cadoc. The second, if not both, stories derive from the Welsh curiosity about place-names; many legends explain their formation (for example, the hunting of the boar, Troit), and in this case a name resembling 'the ford of the pact' (referring to the bargain between Arthur and the saint) was perhaps at the root of the episode.

If Arthur is a tyrant, a little pagan magic is also used to help the saint's reputation, and the principle that the greater the rank of the sinner, the greater the glory of the saint, lies behind the episode. This is equally true of the *Life of St Carannog*, where Arthur has to enlist the saint's aid in order to overcome a serpent.

The *Life of St Gildas*, by another Llancarfan monk, Caradoc, was written about 1130. We have already spoken of its story of the feud between Gildas and Arthur in the previous chapter, as a possible explanation of Gildas' omission of Arthur from the *De Excidio*

Britanniae. In addition to this, there is another incident, apparently imported from secular tradition, which is an early form of the story of Lancelot and Guinevere:

> Gildas . . . arrived at Glastonbury . . . where king Melwas ruled the Summer Country. He was received by the abbot of Glastonbury, and taught the brothers and some of the laity, sowing the seed of the divine doctrines. Here he wrote the histories of the kings of the Britons. Glastonbury is the Town of Glass . . . first named thus in the British tongue. It was besieged by the ruler Arthur with a countless multitude because of Guinevere his wife who had been violated and carried off by the aforesaid wicked king [i.e. Melwas], bringing her there because it was an impenetrable place, defended by reeds, rivers and marsh. The rebellious king [i.e. Arthur] had searched for the queen for a whole year, and had at last heard that she was there. At this news he raised the armies of all Cornwall and Devon, and the enemies prepared for war. Seeing this, the abbot of Glastonbury and his clergy and Gildas the Wise went out between the battle lines and peaceably counselled Melwas their king to return the lady he had carried off. So she was returned, as she should have been, in peace and goodwill.

The influence of Gildas' own work is evident here. Arthur, although he was not one of the tyrants against whom Gildas ranted in vain, is grouped among the wicked princelings of the period. The epithet 'rebellious', however, is a reflection of the earlier story of the quarrel between him and Gildas in the same work, in which he had refused to bow to Gildas' spiritual authority.

But these are only stray episodes and odd fragments of a much greater body of stories. The existence of a much more extensive legend is borne out by twelfth-century writers. Hermann of Laon, writing of a Norman visit to England in 1113, tells us that while in Devon a group of monks were shown 'the chair and oven of that king Arthur famous in the stories of the Britons', and were told 'that that same region had once been Arthur's. William of Malmesbury, in the original version of his *Gesta Regum Anglorum* (*Deeds of the Kings of the English*), 1125, says: 'This is that Arthur of whom the British tales rave today, who plainly deserves not lying fables, but true stories . . .'. Geoffrey of Monmouth whose account of Arthur is the basis of much of the medieval development of his legend, says in the preface to his *History of the Kings of Britain* that stories about Arthur were nowhere recorded in writing, although known and well remembered by many peoples, as if they were written down. The monk Ailred of Rievaulx, in his *Speculum Caritatis* (*Mirror of Charity*), tells how a novice at the monastery (in north-east Yorkshire) was never moved by pious stories, although he had wept over tales which the common folk recited 'about some Arthur [Arcturus] or other' before he had entered the monastery. This is unlikely to refer to Geoffrey's *History of the Kings of Britain*, a Latin work accepted by the historians of the time as accurate, which Ailred, writing in about 1140, could scarcely call 'fables'. It sound more like the work of some wandering story-teller.

How little we know of these story-tellers, and of communications in this period in general, is shown by the distance from which our next evidence comes. From literature, or rather literary fragments, we must turn for a moment to art; and from England we must move to Italy. The work in question is a carving on the north doorway, the 'Porta della Pescheria', of Modena Cathedral. On the semicircular frieze of the archivolt is carved what is generally agreed to be a scene from Arthurian romance. Reading from left to right, we have the following figures, identified by carved labels above them. First, an unnamed knight on horseback, fully armed, follows Isdernus, bareheaded but mounted and equipped with spear and shield. He is preceded by Artus de Bretania, armed and mounted, who is attacking Burmaltus, the latter on foot wielding a hammer, but without mail. A barbican and moated castle at the top of the arch contain a woman, Winlogee, who is accompanied by an unarmed man, Mardoc. To the right of this, an armed knight, Carrado, rides out to attack Galvagin. There follow Galvariun and Che, with their lances on their shoulders. All the last three are armed and mounted: Artus, Galvariun and Che have pennants on the ends of their lances (see Plate 5).

Neither names nor situation will be familiar; but a little interpretation will enable us to recognize them. A castle is being besieged by Arthur (Artus), Ider (Isdernus), a hero of Welsh romance, Gawain (Galvagin), Arthur's nephew, Galeron (Galvariun) and Kay (Che). The defenders are Durmart (Burmaltus), Caradoc (Carrado) and presumably Marrok (Mardoc), all of whom figure in the later Arthurian

31

stories. The woman is Guinevere, Winlogee being a form of her Breton name. The situation as a whole is found in *Durmart le Gallois*, a French romance of c. 1230; but its original is the episode from the *Life of St Gildas* we have quoted earlier.

So far there is nothing remarkable in the carving; a not unfamiliar Arthurian scene, albeit rather far afield. But when it comes to the date of the work, there is much to explain. For although art historians cannot agree as to the exact date of the sculpture, and the style has been variously dated, it is generally believed that this work was executed between 1100 and 1120, *before any Arthurian romances of any sort other than those in Welsh had been written down*. This dating is confirmed by the record of the building of the cathedral, which tells us that a considerable part of the cathedral had been built and the sculptures placed in position by 1106. This probably included the west front, which was usually one of the first parts of a Romanesque cathedral to be built. It has on it carvings so similar in style to those on the 'Porta della Pescheria' that they cannot be more than a decade or two later or earlier. Hence the latest date for the Arthurian frieze is 1130, more than twenty years before the earliest known written romance.

However incredible this sculpture may appear to be, and however difficult to accept, we have to explain how it came to be produced in Italy at a time when we have no recorded legends of any substance about Arthur on his native soil. Such slender evidence as we have already discussed shows that some sort of legend about Arthur was current among popular story-tellers of Wales, Cornwall and Brittany; in fact, among the Celtic races descended from the Britons of Arthur's day. And when the Continental romances of two or three decades later are examined, they are full of Celtic names and incidents. We can find parallels to some of these names and incidents in Welsh stories; but often there are bewildering and quite inexplicable discrepancies in an otherwise recognisable Welsh tale. Many hypotheses have been put forward to cover these facts and weld them into a rational whole, and long and complex arguments have resulted.

On the face of it, only one factor appears to reconcile the three points – Celtic tales, French romances, and Italian sculpture –

1   The earliest poetic reference to Arthur in the early
seventh-century poem *The Gododdin*. These lines,
including the words 'ceni ben ef Arthur' (but he was **no**
Arthur) are from a thirteenth-century manuscript

2   The earliest historical mention of 'Arthur' as a
name: the original manuscript of the seventh-century
Life of St Columba by Adomnan. Arthur's death in
battle against the Miathi is described

3   Page from an early
eleventh-century manuscript
of the *Annales Cambriae*.
The right-hand column
records the battle of Badon
and, as the last entry, the
death of Arthur and Mordred
at the battle of Camlann

4   Page from an early
eleventh-century manuscript
of Nennius' *Historia
Britonum* giving Nennius'
version of Arthur's career

5   Archivolt at Modena Cathedral, c. 1100-10. This is the earliest evidence for romances about Arthur, and shows how widely they were spread by word of mouth before being written down. The scene appears to show, from left to right, Ider and Arthur attacking Burmaltus, who defends a castle containing Wintogel (= Guinevere) and Marduc. On the other side, Caradoc defends the castle against Gawain and 'Galvariun'

6   Another mysterious appearance of Arthur in Italy, from a mosaic in Otranto Cathedral, dated 1166. Otranto, in south-east Italy, was ruled by the Normans in the twelfth century.

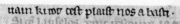

7 Lancelot rides to rescue Queen Guinevere from the stake, from a French manuscript dated 1274

8 Arthur in single combat with the emperor of Rome, from the long romance called the *Roman d'Artus* of the fourteenth century. It is the only romance in which Arthur himself is the hero

9 Gawain fights ten footsoldiers (sergeants) and captures them. From a late thirteenth-century manuscript of the whole 'Vulgate' cycle

10 Iseult discovers that Tristan has killed her betrothed, Morholt, and tries to slay him in his bath. From a fifteenth-century manuscript of the Prose Tristan

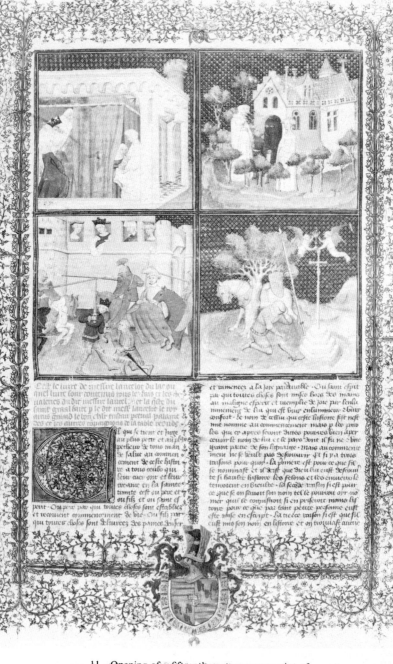

11 Opening of a fifteenth-century manuscript of
Lancelot. Top left: birth of Lancelot. Top right:
Lancelot brought up by the Lady of the Lake.
Bottom left: Lancelot at a tournament.
Bottom right: Lancelot's vision of the Holy Grail

12   Sir Agravain sees the coffin of a knight who
has been slain by treachery, and (right) captures
the brother of the murderer. From *Lancelot*

13 'How the Comte des Broches undertook a
tournament against King Nabor, in which Gawain
took part . . .' from a manuscript of *Lancelot* dated
1344

14 Galahad comes to take his place in the Perilous
Seat, from a fourteenth-century manuscript.

namely, the Bretons. The Bretons came of Celtic stock, and had many points of contact with France and indeed throughout Europe. Records show that they travelled widely, and were found in Wales as well as in France at this time; and it seems that it must have been they who transmitted the tales. This would explain the strange discrepancies between the Welsh originals and the French versions. But there remains one major obstacle: there is no written trace of any Breton version of these legends.

This need not necessarily deter us; for most of the Welsh legends were only recorded in the memory of the bards, and told or sung at feasts. Similarly, the Bretons must have had their bards; their material may well have been the same as the Welsh, but they were free to wander beyond their own borders into France in search of an audience. The mysterious figure of Master Blihis, who appears as author or source in some romances, might be such a travelling poet, though there is evidence to connect him with Wales. The stories told by such bards would have attracted the writers and poets of the newly-developed French language, the vernacular tongue as opposed to the Latin of Church and Court officials, and in much elaborated forms passed into literature proper.

Such, drastically compressed, is the core of the argument in favour of the Breton origin of the French romances. Many minor points support it; Bretons are recorded both in Yorkshire, near the monastery where Ailred of Rievaulx wrote of the 'fables about Arthur', and in northern Italy, on their way to the First Crusade in 1096, near Modena and the carving on the cathedral. The names in the French romances appear to show traces of a double translation, and are closer to Breton than Welsh: Owein ap Urien of the triads appears as Yvain in French and Ivan in Breton, to name but one of many such examples. The Bretons would be more likely to know French tastes, and to cater for them accordingly, whereas the Welsh, while knowing the stories better, were less likely to be able to present them in a popular form. Nor were the Bretons an intellectually backward race: among other major figures of the period of Breton stock we find Peter Abelard and another philosopher, Bernard of Chartres.

On the other hand, we know very little about Welsh contacts

abroad through Norman French culture. None of the evidence comes from areas which were not also subject to Norman influence (except the Modena sculpture); and even this could have been the work of an itinerant northern French craftsman. It is unlikely that any certain answer will ever emerge; two or three lost manuscripts of early French translations of Welsh stories would suffice to fill the gap between *The Mabinogion* and Chrétien de Troyes, and jongleurs or travelling minstrels were just as likely to have been French as Breton. All that is certain is the Celtic origin of the French romances, though many of the details have been added or altered in the process of translation and transmission.

Arthur's period of transition from reality to romance was a long and complex one. He was remembered as a hero by the Welsh bards, who embroidered and added to his legends in their own skilful way, and from Wales the stories were taken either to fellow-Celts in Brittany or direct to France. About the turn of the twelfth century they enjoyed great popularity there, and were spread by the jongleurs and minstrels who wandered from castle to castle reciting at feasts. At these recitals, the French poets seized eagerly on the new material, and fashioned from it the earliest versions of the Arthurian legends that we possess today.

3

Arthur the Emperor

From the title of our next work, Geoffrey of Monmouth's *Historia Regum Britanniae* (*History of the Kings of Britain*) it might seem that we were returning once more to the serious historical side of Arthur's career. But the matter-of-fact title conceals one of the greatest fictitious stories in English literature, one which was to have much influence with succeeding generations, and which encouraged the development of a written legend in no small degree.

Only a few details of the life of its author are known. Geoffrey of Monmouth, or Geoffrey Arthur as he is sometimes called, was born about 1100, of either Welsh or Breton descent. We first hear of him as a witness to charters in or near Oxford from 1129 onwards. He seems to have lived in Oxford, and to have been associated with Robert of Chesney, later Bishop of Lincoln, to whom he dedicated his last work, the *Vita Merlini* (*Life of Merlin*), and with Walter archdeacon of Oxford, who is said to have provided him with the source of the *History*. The link between the three men seems to have been the college of secular canons, St George's, in Oxford, Walter being its provost and Robert one of the six canons. Although Oxford was not yet an established university, Geoffrey, who on two occasions calls himself 'magister', may have held some sort of teaching appointment.

His earliest surviving literary effort, is the *Prophetia Merlini* (*Prophecies of Merlin*), which was later incorporated in the *History of the Kings of Britain* as Book VII, and was completed about 1132–5. He tells us at the beginning of the book that he began the *History* first, intending to deal with the sayings of Merlin later. But stories about Merlin began to circulate from other sources, and he was urged by his friend Alexander, Bishop of Lincoln, and others, to complete this book first. This he did, and the *Prophecies* appeared independently before his major work. The *History of the Kings of Britain* seems to have been started about 1130 and finished shortly after the death of Henry I in 1135. From the dedications we learn that Geoffrey was seeking the patronage of some important figure to secure him an ecclesiastical appointment, but for the time being he was unsuccessful. It was not until after he had written the last of his three known works, the Latin poem on the life of Merlin, in 1148, and dedicated it to Robert of Chesney, recently appointed Bishop of Lincoln, that he gained his object. Although he was ordained priest on 11 February 1152, and before the end of the same month consecrated bishop of St Asaph in Flintshire – probably through Robert's influence – the post was almost certainly a sinecure of the type held by professional writers like himself, and in any case Norman influence in the area was so uncertain that he may never even have visited his diocese. The legend according to which he was buried in the cathedral is certainly without foundation. He died three years after his appointment.

Geoffrey's main interest was not the Church, he entered it merely because it was the most convenient career for a literary man. We have no evidence in his writings of a religious vocation, but in the times and circumstances this is by no means unusual. The greatest of the translators of the *History*, Maistre Wace, was given a canonry at Bayeux in similar fashion as a royal reward for a commissioned work. Far more important than Geoffrey's clerical standing is his Welsh descent. Several of the lives of the saints mentioned in chapter two seem to have been written by south Welsh monks in response to the curiosity of the newly-arrived Normans about the history of the country. It is more than possible that a similar inquiry prompted Geoffrey to produce his great national epic on the Britons.

How much Geoffrey drew on his Welsh sources, and how much on his imagination, is a vexed question. But his two works on Merlin certainly have a strong basis in Welsh literature; before 1100 there is no lack of material about him. Geoffrey himself claims that the prophecies are translations from the Welsh, and this would seem, at least in part, to be true. Even his most hostile critic, William of Newburgh, can find no more scathing remark than that he added much. Some of the story of Merlin comes from Nennius' account of the boy Ambrosius, whose history and prophecies provide the outline for those of Geoffrey's seer. Giraldus Cambrensis, writing at the beginning of the thirteenth century, carefully distinguishes between this Merlin (Merlin Ambrosius) and another Merlin (Merlin Sylvester), a remark which leads us to Geoffrey's original, the prophet Myrddin who figures in some more than usually obscure Welsh poems. From the fragments of his story contained in the latter, we learn that the central characters were Myrddin himself, Gwenddolau, Gwendydd and Rhydderch. In the battle of Arfderydd (probably Arthuret near Carlisle) Rhydderch seems to have killed Myrddin's lord, Gwenddolau. This, and a vision in the sky during the battle, caused Myrddin to go mad. Gwendydd was his sister, but seems to have had some special part in the disaster which we know nothing about. In Geoffrey's *Life of Merlin* we meet all four again. Ganieda (Gwendydd) is in addition the wife of Rodarchus (Rhydderch), a detail which probably came from the lost part of the Welsh story.

Another source for these works comes from Scotland. Myrddin is connected with the Lailoken of certain legends preserved in the *Life of St Kentigern*. Both are associated with Rhydderch, and the Welshman is called 'Llallogan' at one point, suggesting a parallel with the name Lailoken. From these stories came Merlin's link with the Forest of Celidon, as a result of which Merlin Sylvester is sometimes known as Merlin Celidonius.

These legends were embroidered in later French romances, but Geoffrey himself only used them in his last work, for *The Prophecies of Merlin* as their title implies, have little to do with the biography of Merlin, and are in any case mainly based on the utterances of Ambrosius, though some remarks may come from other Welsh and Scottish tradition. The result falls into three parts: prophecies concerning a period in the past for Geoffrey; those concerning the near future for Geoffrey; and a series of apocalyptic scenes. The first part, which would of course be the future for Merlin, is known as *ex post facto* prophecy; the predictions are composed after the event and attributed to someone who is supposed to have lived before it. Hence the references are clear in many instances, in spite of their cryptic form. The sinking of the White Ship in 1120 is alluded to as follows: 'The lion's cubs shall be transformed into fishes of the sea.' Henry I is, of course, the lion: his 'cubs' included the heir, Prince William, his only son, who was drowned in this disaster. Through this type of prophecy Merlin's reputation for accuracy in prediction was established, and Geoffrey goes on to make a number of vague allusions of great ambiguity in the second part. Occasionally he refers to projected schemes which have not yet come to fruition. These sketches of the future become more and more vague until they merge into the third section, the apocalypse, for which Geoffrey used the Bible and possibly classical sources for suitable imagery.

In their proper place in the *History*, these prophecies point forward to its climax in Arthur's reign, and form an integral part of the structure: but they were often copied out separately, and enjoyed a wide independent popularity. Commentaries were numerous; the most elaborate is that once ascribed to Alanus de Insulis, probably in fact by Alan of Tewkesbury, written between 1167 and 1174, from which the quotation at the beginning of this book is taken. Many imitations of the *Prophecies* itself followed, in almost every western European language, until Merlin was recognised from Iceland to Sicily as a prophetic figure of the greatest importance.

But it was not the *Prophecies* alone that made Geoffrey's reputation; it was chiefly the work of which they usually form part, the *History of the Kings of Britain*. This was completed about 1135–6. The opening dedication shows clearly that Geoffrey was seeking favour with prominent men, for there are three versions of it, each corresponding to a change in the political situation. The earliest of these is that which names Robert of Gloucester alone. Robert had supported Matilda immediately after the death of Henry I, but when the crown went to Stephen, he swore allegiance to the latter. Geoffrey seems to have been inspired by this new political development to add the name of Stephen's chief supporter, Waleran de Beaumont, who had often been connected with Robert in earlier years. When Robert was on more intimate terms with the King, Geoffrey moved him into second place, and put Stephen at the head with the attributes formerly given to Robert, and omitted Waleran. This combination of Stephen and Robert could not have been later than April 1138, for in that month Robert reverted finally to his former allegiance to Matilda. It is possible that Geoffrey then used the single dedication to Robert once again, for we should expect to find one to Stephen alone if Geoffrey had abandoned Robert's side. This is the most obvious of Geoffrey's attempts to ingratiate himself with the ruling classes; but we shall find other, more subtle means used in the actual historical part of the work.

What were Geoffrey's sources? How historically reliable is his narrative? And what was the 'very ancient book in the British tongue' which he claims to have used? All three questions can best be answered by a study of the last point. In the dedication Geoffrey states clearly that he used such a book, which related the histories of all the British kings, from Brutus to Cadwallader, and that it was given to him by Walter, archdeacon of Oxford. However, this book is now completely lost; we have nothing even remotely corresponding to it. But there is almost unanimous agreement among scholars that it never existed in the first place in the form indicated by Geoffrey. The invocation of a lost souce to give authority to a fictitious work is by no means unusual in medieval literature; for example, the group of romances about Troy were based on an imaginary work by one Dares, which had a considerable history attached to its discovery. And Geoffrey's *History* is romantic rather than factual history; we need not therefore accuse him of actual fraud. Let us say rather that here is an early example of a literary formula which has since been widely used, and that Geoffrey himself did not expect any great historical weight to be given to the result. We have no definite evidence of his intentions, and the nature of his other works would indicate a bent for the fictional rather than the historical. In an age which lacked the historical evidence or critical method of today, and which perpetuated the error made by Henry of Huntingdon in regarding the *History* as an essay in history with serious foundation, no sharp distinction was made by most historical writers between fact and fancy; Geoffrey was merely less scrupulous than many of his contemporaries in making this division.

But this does not mean to say that he used no other source than his own imagination. Although he has in places concocted entire histories out of almost nothing, he restrained himself enough to give the result a quite false air of reality that made these stories generally accepted as accurate in outline, if not in detail, until the eighteenth century. Just as Arthur, as Geoffrey depicts him, is unhistorical, so is much of the rest. Brutus of Troy, the supposed founder of the British race and kingdom, Lud, from whom London was said to have got its name, King Lear, of Shakespearian fame, Caesar's three attempts to conquer Britain, and final success only through treachery on the part of a British noble – all these are the products of Geoffrey's brilliant imagination working on a name or an odd reminiscence. Against this, we find only occasional touches of history: Caractacus appears, though Boadicea is conspicuously absent; the appeal of the Britons to Aetius is historical fact, as are also some of the details after Arthur's time. For the period after the withdrawal of the Roman legions, Geoffrey draws on what was at the time accepted history, Nennius' *History of the Britons,* and uses it up to the beginning of Arthur's career. Other details show that he knew a number of Welsh legends. For example, the name of Arthur's father, Uther, may be due to a misunderstanding of 'Arthur mab uthr', Arthur the terrible, as Arthur son of Uther. Arthur's weapons are derived from various such Welsh stories: Caliburnus, his sword, better known as Excalibur, is identical with Caledfwlch in the Welsh, his lance Ron the same as Rhongomyniad, both found as his weapons in *Culhwch and Olwen.* The name of his shield arises out of a confusion with that of his ship: Pridwen is a ship in the poem *The Spoils of Annwfn,* but appears as a shield in Geoffrey's account.

Geoffrey's account of Arthur's career is the climax of the *History* and occupies about one third of the whole book. It is foreshadowed in Merlin's marvellous prophecies which immediately precede it; and it is with Merlin's supernatural aid that Arthur is born. Uther falls violently in love with Igerna, wife of his enemy, Gorlois of Cornwall, and is magically transformed (by Merlin) into the latter's likeness. He enters the castle of Tintagel in Gorlois' absence, and begets Arthur by her. On his return, he learns that Gorlois has been killed a few hours earlier, and therefore marries Igerna at the earliest opportunity. Arthur thus enjoys the benefit of being miraculously and yet almost legitimately conceived. On his father's death, he succeeds to the throne, being then fifteen, and he is crowned by Archbishop Dubricius. His first campaign is against the Saxons, who had caused his father's death by poisoning him. He defeats their leader, Colgrim, in a series of battles based on the twelve described by Nennius. Arthur's chief allies are the Bretons, who play an important part throughout his reign, and whose leader Hoel is second only to Arthur himself.

Having defeated the Saxons with Hoel's assistance, he settles the internal affairs of his kingdom, and marries Guanhumara, daughter of a Cornish nobleman, who is of course the Gwenhwyfar of the Welsh and the Guinevere of Malory. His ambitions now rise to an imperial plane, and without any apparent effort he proceeds to conquer, or receive homage from, large areas of northern Europe. Ireland is his first objective, and its conquest is swiftly followed by that of Iceland, Gothland and the Orkneys. Norway is overcome and given to his brother-in-law; Dacia (Denmark), Aquitaine and Gaul have to be subjugated before his appetite is temporarily sated.

He then returns to Britain to hold his Whitsuntide crown-wearing; and it is here that Geoffrey waxes most eloquent over the glories of the Court. However, immediately the festivities are concluded, there arrive messengers from Lucius Hiberus, the Roman Emperor, demanding tribute on the grounds that Britain was once a Roman province. Arthur convenes a council of kings, who unanimously agree that the only possible answer to so outrageous a demand is to march on Rome at once.

The kingdom is entrusted to Mordred and the army prepares to embark at Hamo's Port (Southampton). On the night before departure, Arthur has a foreboding dream which presages the coming struggle between himself and Lucius, or, according to another interpretation, between himself and a giant. He proceeds to France, landing at Barfleur, where he hears that a giant has carried off and killed Hoel's niece. He therefore makes a detour to Mont Saint Michel, and disposes of the monster. Continuing his march to Burgundy, he hears that the Romans are encamped hard by. He sets off in pursuit, and, after various skirmishes, engages the main body of the army in a wooded valley near Langres. Lucius is killed and the Romans defeated, though not without considerable losses on the British side; notable among the slain are Kay and Bedivere.

Having thus cleared the way to Rome, Arthur is preparing to march south again, when he hears that Mordred has proved treacherous. He has usurped the crown and is about to marry Guinevere, having falsely spread the news that Arthur is dead. On learning this, Arthur immediately returns to Britain, dispatching the bodies of Lucius and various senators to Rome in lieu of the tribute.

At this point, Geoffrey begins a new book, changes his style and deals with the remainder of Arthur's reign in one-tenth of the space allotted to the Roman campaign. When Arthur lands in Britain, Mordred retires with his forces into Cornwall, where Arthur meets and engages him. In this final battle, Mordred is killed with almost all his followers; but Arthur's forces suffer no less, Arthur himself being taken to the mysterious Avalon for his wounds to be healed. Guinevere retires to a convent and the kingdom passes to Constantine. Geoffrey's narrative becomes terse and seemingly purely factual.

The borderline between Geoffrey's own invention and the legendary material he has incorporated is hard to define. We have already compared the degree of historical fact and looked at the sources of some of the names he uses; but these are by no means so elusive as the incidental stories. The main outline of Arthur's career in the *History* is Geoffrey's own; but how much of the detail came from his fertile brain? One incident, a curious chapter on marvellous ponds in Britain, which Arthur describes to Hoel at the end of the Saxon campaign, is drawn from Nennius' *Marvels*. Similarly, the episode of Mont Saint Michel has little to do with the main military campaign; both this and another giant-killing recounted by Arthur afterwards come from a totally different atmosphere of personal strength and valour, and are found independent of Arthur himself in later Welsh legend. It seems as though Geoffrey had made use of all the possible material in the Welsh traditions, and only invented new stories as a last resort. Even the idea of Arthur's expedition to Gaul may be a dim memory of the several usurpers who set out from Britain to claim the imperial title during the Roman occupation.

But Geoffrey has done a great deal more than simply combine the Welsh legendary and historical portraits of Arthur. He has formed an entirely new portrait as a result of his alterations; and a study of these changes will show us what he intended the new Arthur to represent, as well as revealing some of his other motives in writing the *History*.

We have already noted the remark in a variant manuscript of Nennius which says of Arthur that 'though there were many more noble than he, yet was he twelve times chosen commander'. Geoffrey takes this hint of mystery about his origins and uses it to elaborate his story. He may have thought of the two chief figures in contemporary romances, Charlemagne and Alexander. It is the latter's biography that seems to have supplied the idea of a magical birth involving disguises and transformations. Alexander's father in these stories was not Philip, his mother's husband, but one Nectanebus, a wizard and exiled king of Egypt, who arrived in Macedonia during Philip's absence and fell in love with his wife Olympiades. He told her that the god Ammon would come to her in the shape of a dragon which would then turn into a man; and a great hero would be born to her. However, Philip returns unexpectedly, but consents to receive the strange visitor and then retire. It is in fact Nectanebus himself who arrives under this disguise, and in due course Alexander is born. Both these stories may come from that of Jupiter and Amphitryon, though there is an Irish parallel in the story of the birth of the hero Mongan. The general idea of some mystery attached to the birth of a great hero is present in all three, and Geoffrey uses the story to raise Arthur to the status of Alexander and Hercules.

The other striking development is that of Arthur's Continental and Scandinavian empire. This is not difficult to trace. At the time when Geoffrey was writing, just before the death of Henry I, the rulers of Britain were beginning to think once more in terms of overseas dominions of which Britain would be the centre. Geoffrey, by taking an earlier empire of which Britain had been the centre, and combining it with that of Charlemagne, the other great contemporary hero of romance besides Alexander, was merely catering for current taste and interest. The first empire was that of Canute, who would have represented to Geoffrey what Napoleon I would to a Frenchman of today in terms of distance in time. Canute had ruled all the lands in Arthur's empire except for those in France, which were Charlemagne's, and Ireland, over which he had, however, claimed suzerainty.

Arthur's campaigns against the Saxons are described at great length. Parallels can be draw between the English campaigns of William I and those of Arthur. But the main source of inspiration seems to have remained Nennius, from whom eight of the battles are adopted directly, albeit under Geoffrey's interpretation of their sites (evidence that the identity of these was already in doubt). Nonetheless, the events immediately following the campaigns offer a remarkable resemblance. In 1069 William spent Christmas at York, which had been laid waste by Normans and Danes in turn. He appointed a new archbishop, the former prelate having recently died, and drew up plans for the general restoration of the city. When compared with Arthur's actions, the connection cannot be lightly set aside. Arthur is specifically stated to have been at York for Christmas, and he similarly appoints a new archbishop, though Geoffrey adds a realistic detail by making Arthur's personal chaplain the new prelate.

On considering these sources of inspiration, we begin to get an idea of Geoffrey's object in writing the *History*. He seems to be attempting to provide the Britons with an emperor-hero to whose golden age they could look back with pride. France had Charlemagne; the Greeks, Alexander; and the Saxons, Beowulf and kindred heroes. Arthur's history is modelled, as has been shown, on the first two; but Geoffrey is no slavish imitator. It is the concept of the emperor-hero that he has adopted, rather than minor details. In fact, he succeeds in incorporating much national material in the execution of this idea, and gives it a suitably British outlook. All these imperial chronicles lie on the borderline of history and romance, and Geoffrey is merely more obviously inclined to fiction than the others.

It is a conscious attempt to create a national epic, in the same way as the *Aeneid,* or, closer parallel, the *Franciad* of Pierre de Ronsard.

Geoffrey's other object may have been to provide politically useful precedents. Even if his work as a whole is unhistorical, there is enough accurate material in it to make fact and fiction hard to distinguish, as we have seen. So his work could be quoted with reasonable safety in cases where a precedent was required. Brittany and Scotland are two examples of this. The Bretons play a considerable part in the *History,* but are rarely found in connection with Arthur elsewhere. If we look at the contemporary political situation of Brittany and England, we shall find a possible reason for this bias on Geoffrey's part. A tenuous claim to overlordship of Brittany had been advanced by the Normans since the days of William the Conqueror, and this was confirmed only in 1113. The Duchy of Brittany was, however, still poised between independence and the feudal suzerainty of Normandy, and in any case was a valuable ally. So a reminder of the connection between the two countries was likely to go down well in the Norman Court, and a little flattery of the Bretons would be regarded favourably. As for Scotland, Edward III in a letter of 1301 to the Pope, actually quotes the *History* in support of his claim to it. Geoffrey, albeit rather belatedly, seems to have been successful in his object.

The question of the large role assigned to the Bretons in the *History* is interesting, for they vanish completely from Arthurian romance except in those works directly based on Geoffrey. He seems to have had some special, possibly personal, reason for giving them this part. The idea of creating a precedent has already been mentioned. It has also been suggested that he was of Breton, not Welsh blood, and his sympathies do seem to be inclined towards the Bretons at the expense of the Welsh. The latter appear in a none too favourable role in the more recent part of the *History,* after the end of Arthur's reign, but it is possible that many of his hostile remarks come from Gildas. Finally, it is conceivable that the 'very ancient book' which he quotes as the source of the *History* may have been a volume of British genealogies from Brittany, and hence with a Breton bias; though on balance this famous volume is more likely to have been fictitious.

Just as contemporary politics provide Geoffrey with some ideas for his narrative, so he draws on contemporary life for details of sixth-century manners and morals, though we should in any case be foolish to expect any attempt at historical realism on Geoffrey's part. On every page, we find customs which would have been entirely out of place in the historical period in which Geoffrey places Arthur's Court. As far as the Court itself is concerned, the most important passage is that describing his crown-wearing at the City of Legions immediately after his campaigns in Gaul against the Romans. The city is here described at length; its churches of St Julius and St Aaron, its convent of canons and college of philosophers, until the magnificence of the Court itself makes even the loquacious Geoffrey pause for words. He can hardly be thinking of the English Court of the twelfth century as he describes this splendour; and a few lines further on, he relates a custom which at once betrays the source of his inspiration. When it comes to the church ceremony, the women go to a separate church; afterwards they hold their own banquet, at the same time as that of the men. These customs have a strong eastern flavour; and the only place where they were combined with Christianity was at Constantinople, a favourite stopping-place for the returning Crusader or pilgrim. It was regarded as the most luxurious city in the Christian world, and it is obviously the model for Geoffrey's City of Legions. Once again, Arthur has risen with remarkable swiftness to the heights of glory from a relative obscurity.

For one of the earliest writers of fiction in the Middle Ages, Geoffrey succeeds remarkably well. But in one thing his touch is not so sure, due to his largely scholarly background. The methods of warfare he describes throughout the *History* are strangely inconsistent; they correspond with no known tactics or equipment, and yet occasionally the latest developments of Geoffrey's own times appear. He seems to have drawn his descriptions from very indirect reports which he cannot really have understood.

The *History of the Kings of Britain* is the greatest single contribution to Arthurian romance. It provided the entire historical part of the story of Arthur, and was more extensively known and used by later writers than any other part of the legend. It is a plausible account, and therein lies Geoffrey's greatest achievement. He produced an historical romance, which, whether he intended it or not, was lifelike enough to be taken by his successors as history for some six hundred years after his death. Up to the beginning of the nineteenth century it was on Geoffrey of Monmouth's story, rather than on Malory's, that the English conception of Arthur was founded.

As an author, Geoffrey had an immediate success by medieval standards. Since the spread of written works depended on the laborious hand-copying of manuscripts, reputations in the literary field were slow in the making, but the *History* was accepted and enthusiastically read by most historians of the time, and there was very little opposition to it. William of Newburgh was the first writer to criticise it sharply, at the end of the twelfth century. In the introduction to his *Historia Rerum Anglicarum* (*History of English Affairs*), he attacks Geoffrey's excessive praise of the British race, his stories about Arthur and Merlin (which had of course been Geoffrey's own largest contribution) and his acceptance of the 'Breton hope' of Arthur's return implied in the departure of Arthur to Avalon in the *History*, and developed in the later *Life of Merlin*. Giraldus Cambrensis, while often citing the *History* as though it were reliable, also tells a story of a man plagued by evil spirits, by which he was able to pick out false passages in books. When St John's Gospel was placed on his breast, the spirits vanished, but when by way of experiment it was replaced by 'Geoffrey Arthur's book' they returned, more horrible and numerous than ever before. He thus implies that he realised the true nature of the work.

But most chroniclers and historical writers followed Geoffrey without question. Henry of Huntingdon, in a letter to a certain Warinus in 1139, gives a summary of it to supplement his own Saxon history, and declares his astonishment at finding the work, which he had seen at Bec in Normandy, on his way home from Rome. Ailred of Beverley, about 1150, was the first to incorporate it into the standard form of historical work of the period, the monastic chronicle, although he does question some parts and rejects others. Some fifty other chroniclers writing in Latin used it in the years up to 1420 to a greater or lesser extent, and it acquired the standing of the accepted authority on the period for British history.

Nor were the poets slow to adopt it. Within two decades, two translations of Geoffrey had appeared in French, and within half a century a Middle English version, taken from the French, followed, in addition to the numerous chronicle abridgements. We no longer possess the first of the French versions, by one Geoffrey Gaimar, but we know something of it from his other work, *Lestoire des Engles* (*The History of the English*) which forms a sequel to it, As far as we can tell, it must have been completed within a decade or so of the original, *c.* 1145–50.

Gaimar's work was, however, rapidly superseded by Maistre Wace's *Roman de Brut*, probably a much superior work from the literary point of view. Wace was born in Jersey in about 1100, and in his youth lived at Caen, where he studied for some time, completing his education in the Ile de France. On his return to Caen, he wrote his first 'romanz' or tales in verse, including some saints' lives. Before writing the *Roman de Brut*, he seems to have visited southern England, possibly through a connection between the two great monasteries at Caen and Sherborne. In 1155, just twenty years after the *History of the Kings of Britain* had been completed by Geoffrey, Wace finished his version of it in French, we learn from his English translator, Layamon, that a copy was given to Queen Eleanor, whose husband, Henry II, had ascended the English throne in the previous year. Wace soon received a commission from the King to write a history of the dukes of Normandy, and he started this, the *Roman de Rou*, in 1160. In 1169, he was appointed to a canonry at Bayeux as a token of royal favour, but since he had still not finished the commissioned work in 1174, Henry asked another poet, Maistre Beneeit, to complete it. Wace must have died shortly after 1175, when his name is found in records for the last time.

The *Roman de Brut*, so named after Brutus, whom Geoffrey of Monmouth made the founder of Britain[1] is largely based on the *History of the Kings of Britain*, though from a manuscript which contained a slightly different version from any that have come down to us. Much of the apparent expansion (from 6,000 lines of Latin

48

prose to 15,000 of French verse) is due to the shortness of the verse line. But Wace has treated his material with some freedom, like many medieval translators. His personal knowledge of southern England led him to make some alterations, especially in the account of the campaign against the Saxons. The French literary tradition supplied him with the element of courtly love, which is absent from Geoffrey, and there is a definitely romantic tone to the work as a whole, in contrast to Geoffrey's drier and more historical approach. The same contrast appears in Wace's use of similes and direct speech, heightening the dramatic and emotional effect. The sea and nautical affairs, scarcely noticeable in Geoffrey, are much to the fore in the *Brut*, possibly because of Wace's childhood environment in Jersey. Lastly, and somewhat surprisingly, there is a rational and critical attitude on Wace's part towards the prophecies of Merlin, which he omits on the ground that they are entirely unintelligible, and he also reduces Merlin's role elsewhere.

But Wace's departures from the main outline of the story are few and far between. He seems either to have been ignorant of Gaimar's earlier French version, or to have ignored his work intentionally, as there is nothing to indicate a double rewriting of Geoffrey. There is, however, one major addition in the Arthurian section of the work, which was to become one of the central ideas of Arthurian romance, Wace relates how Arthur, because his barons could not agree on an order of precedence in seating, 'made the Round Table, of which the Bretons tell many a tale'. It is probable, although disputed, that the Round Table does in fact come from Celtic tradition, and the Bretons may well have been Wace's immediate source. Most of Wace's other additions come from classical legend or local tradition and this highly unusual idea is not in keeping with his normal level of invention.

It was in Wace's work that Arthur himself reached his widest recognition as a poetical hero. Later works might be more popular, or magnify Arthur to a greater extent, but the two factors never coincided again as they do here. No less than twenty-four manuscripts of the *Roman de Brut* survive, and, even if this figure palls beside the mass of manuscripts of its original, it is more than any other medieval French work save one. From it, all other subsequent chronicles of the legendary history of Britain were known as Bruts, and several of these fall within our scope.

The first of these is also the first English vernacular version of the Arthurian legend of which we have record. It is the *Brut* of Layamon, who, as he himself tells us, was parish priest of Areley Regis on the upper reaches of the Severn in Worcestershire. His name (pronounced Lawman) indicates Scandinavian origin, but it is unlikely that he was of Norse-Irish stock, as has been suggested. He completed the *Brut*, his only known work, between 1189–99.

It is a translation from Wace's French from beginning to end, in spite of his claim in the introduction that he had used an English translation of Bede and 'the book of SS Albin and Augustine' as well as the *Roman de Brut*. Most of the additional material is his own, and the result is a total length of 32,000 lines, or twice that of the French version. Just under one-third is concerned with Arthur. Once again, the expansion is in the details rather than in the basic framework of the story. He uses simile extensively and effectively: dead knights in the river Avon are depicted as 'steel fishes lying in the stream . . . their scales float like gold-painted shields, their fins float as if they were spears'. Less rewarding is his use of set phrases which recur with a particular character or situation, a device borrowed from the kennings of Anglo-Saxon literature. His vocabulary is largely Saxon, with not more than two hundred romance words in the whole work, and he has inherited a great variety of synonyms from earlier poets.

In Layamon, the influence of chivalry is entirely lacking. His alterations tend indeed to be in the other direction; the atmosphere is closer to the Welsh tradition which had been Geoffrey of Monmouth's starting point. He explains and simplifies situations rather than making them more complex, as would be only natural for a writer whose audience was the common people rather than the royal Court. Although the French romances were in full spate, there is no trace of any of the later heroes, and the native characters retain their original qualities: Kay is still the brave and valiant knight of Welsh legend, and shares with Bedivere many of the adventures, which are military rather than knightly. Gawain is second only to the king, while Hoel's considerable part in the *History of the Kings of Britain* has been drastically reduced. Merlin's role is also a minor one, and the impact of his appearances is lessened. It is Arthur, and Arthur alone, who has any real importance, his character here reaches its zenith. He is neither the somewhat crude and vigorous leader of the Welsh tales – although it is to the barbaric rather than the aesthetic that his splendour inclines – nor the *roi fainéant* of lascivious tendencies found in some French romances. His courage, generosity, sincerity and leadership are all brought out; but they are seen through the eyes of a simpler culture, and are brought into line with the writer's general attitude. This is less refined and literary in style than that of his sources, as might be expected, and markedly less civilised altogether. Thus Arthur, although he laments his own fallen knights with great tenderness, is ferocious towards his enemies in a way that seems distinctly unappealing today. Yet this ferocity was commonplace in Layamon's time, and examples can be found everywhere in its popular tales and art: the doom paintings in almost every church in the country were scarcely less savage in spirit than Arthur's exultation over the dead Saxon leader, Colgrim: 'Even if you desired to go to heaven, you shall go to hell, ever to remain there, never to return.' However, even this barbaric streak cannot detract from the magnificence of Layamon's portrait of Arthur.

The account of the Round Table is an important expansion of Wace's story. Layamon tells us how, at a Christmas feast attended by seven kings' sons with seven hundred knights, a quarrel over precedence arose, and several of them were slain in the ensuing fight. When Arthur went to Cornwall shortly afterwards, he met a carpenter from foreign lands who had heard about the incident and offered to make him a table which could be carried anywhere, and at which sixteen hundred men could sit without one being higher than the next. He was provided with materials, and completed the table in six weeks. The association with Cornwall and the miraculous nature of the table point to a possible origin in an Irish saga, and certainly to a Celtic source.

One element that at first appears to conflict with a heroic conception of Arthur is the element of faery successfully introduced by

Layamon. A natural part of many stories familiar to his audience, it adds an aura of mystery and of greater, hidden powers at work. Both at his birth and death, Arthur is attended by supernatural beings – 'elves' fails to translate the Saxon 'elven' adequately. These, it is implied, give him their support throughout his life, and Argante, their queen, carries him away at his death. The closing scene of Arthur's life in Layamon is only rivalled by that in Malory:

> 'Constantine, I leave you my kingdom, guard my Britons, and see that they keep the laws that I have given them. I myself will go to Avalon, where Argante, queen of faery, has her dwelling. She will heal my wounds, for her draughts make men whole again. And then I will return to reign joyfully over my kingdom again.' And as he spoke, a little boat came over the waves, in which sat two ladies, richly dressed, and they bore Arthur at once to the boat, and laid him gently down, and the boat sped away. But the British folk say that Arthur yet lives in Avalon, held by a magic spell, and they await his return.

Layamon alters another supernatural event in Geoffrey's last chapter. This is Arthur's dream presaging the conflict between him and Lucius Hiberus. In Layamon's version a different dream is described, and its import is different, for it foreshadows the treachery of Mordred and Guinevere. It is also more dramatically conceived: Arthur is sitting on the roof of his hall with Gawain, when Mordred appears with a throng of men and starts to cut down the posts supporting the building. Guinevere aids him by tearing off the roof. The building collapses, killing Gawain, but Arthur himself escapes, and beheads Mordred and the queen, to find himself alone on a wild moor. A golden lion approaches; he mounts it and is carried down to the seashore. The lion starts to swim out to sea with him, but he loses his grip on the lion's mane and is only rescued by a giant fish, which deposits him once again on the shore. This episode, in the vein of symbolism found in the *Prophecies of Merlin* is typical of the medieval attitude towards dreams: writers delighted in using such vivid scenes to foreshadow coming events in their narrative.

So it is in Layamon's *Brut* that Arthur reaches his personal apogee as a great emperor whose own deeds are the focal point of the story. Nor is this unexpected: Geoffrey was an ambitious writer in the historical tradition, Wace a courtly chronicler: both were trying to please and obtain favour of the highest in the land. Layamon was a humble story-teller far more concerned with his actual tale; much more forthright in his approval or disapproval of character, and lacking any interest in the subtle psychological analysis of the French writers, as is shown by his treatment of Guinevere; her transfer of affections to Mordred is abrupt, and takes place only when dictated by the plot. But Layamon was also working in a relatively obscure tradition – English had not yet come to literary maturity, and the *Brut* never gained the popularity of its predecessors, its influence on later writers is negligible. So later chroniclers' accounts are largely drawn from Wace or Geoffrey.

The most important of these later works is more poetic than historical. Known as the Thornton (from the name of the copyist, Robert Thornton) or alliterative *Morte Arthure*, to distinguish it from the totally different Harleian or stanzaic *Le Mort Arthur*, it is one of the finest of the English Arthurian poems. Written between 1350 and 1400 in the north of England, its rich and unusual vocabulary has been the chief obstacle to its appreciation in modern times. Furthermore, the present copy seems to have been much altered during transcription, and perhaps even written down from memory by Thornton.

It is chiefly based on the *History of the Kings of Britain*, with some additions from later works, including the version of Wace on which Layamon's *Brut* relied, some *chansons de geste*, notably that of Fierabras (from which the encounter of Gawain and Priamus is drawn) and finally the romances of which Alexander is the hero. The vivid dramatisation that has taken place, in a different idiom, but on the same lines as that carried out by Wace and Layamon, requires no other source than the anonymous writer's own imagination. Many other departures from the original can be explained by what may be termed the contemporary reference process. Just as Geoffrey of Monmouth drew on events and politics of his own times, and thus created parallels between his portrait of Arthur and the Norman kings, so the author of the *Morte Arthure* has to some extent modelled Arthur and his deeds on the Plantagenets and their campaigns. Nor was he the last to use this process, for in Malory's portrait of the same king are traces of Henry v.[2] A few instances from the poem may be used in illustration. The scene of the great battle against Lucius Hiberus exactly resembles that of Crécy. A sea fight is introduced, which appears to be a description of that off Winchelsea against the Spanish fleet in 1350; the author mentions Spaniards where the sense would require Romans, and this may well be a slip of the pen. Mordred and Roger Mortimer have several points in common, and the charges brought against Mordred are similar to those of Mortimer's impeachment. Hoel's niece, who in Geoffrey played a very minor role, becomes Duchess of Brittany and niece to Arthur, thus presenting an analogy with Jeanne de Montfort, who was similarly related to Edward III, and held the same title. Lorraine, where most of Arthur's battles are fought, is probably meant to be the Brittany of Edward III's campaigns in 1340–5. But Arthur's imperial ambitions cannot be paralleled in Edward's career, and the fact that Arthur is about to be crowned when he is forced to return[3] is also an entirely novel idea.

Other additions are purely incidental, but nonetheless interesting. Arthur's route through Italy follows that given in the thirteenth-century itinerary by one Adam of Domerham in general outline, but mention of places not included in that work implies a more intimate knowledge of the country, either on the part of the writer himself or of one of his acquaintances. Few travellers other than diplomatic emissaries made the journey from England to Rome, but in 1350 a party of four hundred pilgrims went there for the jubilee year celebrations. It is reasonable to assume that either the writer or his informant were among them, especially since the whole idea of Arthur's invasion of Italy is found only in this one work.

Before Arthur is forced to abandon his imperial pretensions, he has a dream in which he sees himself as one of the great emperors, bearing the symbols of imperial coronation, and seated on one of the nine chairs of Fortune's wheel. He reaches the highest point of the wheel, and, like his predecessors, is dashed down at the next turn of it. This symbol of earthly vanity and mortality is common in medieval literature, but good use of it is made here. Finally, on his return from the Continent, Arthur engages Mordred in a sea-fight on the beach, in which Gawain is killed. Both Arthur and Mordred speak movingly of his greatness. The final battle follows, and Arthur, although victorious, is mortally wounded and buried at Glastonbury.

This is one of the great medieval epic poems, but the distance of time has made its language too difficult for readers today, while Malory is still accessible without too much labour. Malory draws heavily on the *Morte Arthure* in the early part of his work, but even he rephrases it extensively. So it is his version that is famous, while the original languishes in obscurity. But the earlier poem has many merits: strong characterisation, which lends dignity to Mordred, often a mere villain, and enables him to command our sympathy; a sense of inescapable tragedy, again shared by Mordred, who is reluctant to become regent; powerful oratory in the speeches, particularly in Arthur's eulogy of the dead Gawain, who appears here in his early and untarnished character as Arthur's chief warrior. And there is a surging strength in the verse, particularly in the battle scenes: the following translation can only hint at the vigour of the original, evoking the confusion of a sea-fight:

Then the mariners gather, and masters of ships
Merrily each of the mates talks to the others,
Speaking in their language, telling how things were,
Drawing bundles on board, tying up sails,
Crowding on canvas, battening down hatches,
Brandishing brown steel, blowing their trumpets;
One stands stiffly at the bows, another steers aft;
Gliding over the water, the fighting begins.
The waving wind rises out of the west,
Blows its burly breath into men's sails,
Hurling together the stately ships
So that prows and strakes burst asunder;
The stern strikes so sharply against the stem
That the planks of the rudder are dashed in pieces!
Great ships and small crash against one another.
Grappling irons are thrown out, as they should be,
The stays are hewn down that held up the masts.
There is keen strife and cracking ships.
Great ships of battle are crushed into pieces!

The *Morte Arthure* is the last important piece in the tradition which treats Arthur's story in chronicle fashion. After it come only a brief doggerel account of his career, precise and rather pedantic, attached to a Latin chronicle, and a number of entries in chronicles proper. There had been poetic versions of the bulk of Geoffrey's work by various writers, notably Robert of Gloucester, Peter Langtoft, and Robert Mannyng. The last of these, best known for his lively book *Handlyng Synne*, produced a good version of Arthur's history, but it does not compare well with the *Morte Arthure*.

Writers whose country had supposedly been conquered by Arthur naturally took a less flattering view of his exploits. Thus in the Scottish chronicles, from John of Fordun in the fourteenth century onwards, Arthur is regarded with suspicion; Hector Boece's version of the story in 1528 is the most extreme, making Mordred the rightful heir who is supplanted by Arthur. But more serious historical doubts were being put forward about Geoffrey's account. Robert Fabyan, in his *New Chronicles* at the end of the fifteenth century, questioned his accuracy for the first time in three centuries, and omitted the romantic and supernatural elements of the *History*. A modified account of Geoffrey's work prevailed until Polydore Vergil took the critical approach further than the mood of the times warranted in his *Historia Anglica* of 1534. As a result, several writers came out in defence of Geoffrey, and it was not until the advent of serious historical criticism in the seventeenth century that the obviously legendary parts were rejected. Even then, Geoffrey's version was so well established that it was the end of the eighteenth century before the whole outline was labelled as historically unacceptable. It says much for the merits of the *History* that it was able to deceive historians for six hundred years into a false view of the period it covered. The romantic history of Geoffrey of Monmouth has permanently coloured our idea of Arthur; and its writer could hardly have hoped for greater success than this.

4

Arthur and Avalon

Arthur in the twelfth and thirteenth centuries was not only the central figure of a vast literature, a subject for poets and their patrons; there had also grown up around him a widespread belief that he would one day return as the saviour of the British peoples, to lead them once more to their ancient supremacy over their island. As early as the seventh or eighth century, in a Welsh poem entitled *Verses on the Graves of the Heroes*, we find that he is regarded as something of an enigma in this respect: 'Concealed till Doomsday is the grave of Arthur.'[1] More definite in content is the incident in a French work by one Hermann of Laon, concerning a visit to Britain by some French canons with a holy relic:

> In the town called Bodmin ... a certain man with a withered hand kept watch in the presence of the relic in order to benefit from its holiness. But, just as the Bretons are wont to quarrel with the French about King Arthur, the same man began to argue with one of our companions, Haganellus, related to the archdeacon Guido of Laudun, saying that Arthur was still alive. No little tumult arose out of this; several men burst into the church carrying weapons, and had not Algardus, head of the clergy, interrupted, blood might well have been shed. Since we believed that the quarrel which had taken place in front of the relic displeased our Lord, the man with the withered hand who had caused the tumult about Arthur did not recover his health.

This incident occurred in 1113, some twenty years before the first major Arthurian work was written down, and is valuable testimony to the currency of stories by word of mouth about Arthur. The fierceness with which this belief in his return was supported is also noteworthy; it argues a well-established tradition, and indeed within a few years this tradition seems to have assumed the proportions of a political force, invoked in Welsh rebellions against the English. We have other evidence of such stories around this period, notably that of William of Malmesbury. Speaking of the discovery of Gawain's grave some forty years earlier, he says, 'But the tomb of Arthur is nowhere to be seen, for which reason the dirges of old relate that he is to come again.'

Geoffrey of Monmouth, as one would expect, has heard of the tradition, and makes use of it, but with the introduction of a new element. Arthur is described as being borne away to Avalon. We learn from the *Life of Merlin* that this is a sort of 'other-world' Garden of the Hesperides, an Isle of Apples presided over by nine fays, of whom Morgan is the chief. The Avalon-Isle of Apples identification was to recur later; but let us follow the fortunes of the legend of Arthur's return until then.

Henry of Huntingdon, in his summary of Geoffrey in a letter to a certain Warinus in 1139, uses similar words to those of William of Malmesbury, '. . . he himself received so many wounds that he fell; although his kinsmen the Britons deny that he was mortally wounded and seriously expect he will come again'. An independent witness is that of Alan of Tewkesbury in 1170, in his commentary on Merlin's prophecies,

> And he continued: His departure will be obscured by doubt, which is indeed true, for there are today varying opinions as to his life and death. If you do not believe me, go to the kingdom of Armorica, that is, lesser Britain, and preach in the villages and market places that Arthur the Briton died as other men die; and then, if you escape unharmed, for you will be either cursed or stoned by your hearers, you will indeed discover that Merlin the prophet spoke truly when he said that Arthur's departure would be obscured by doubt.

Other followers of Geoffrey echo these words in variously embellished forms; the finest version is probably that of Layamon, which has already been quoted.

But Geoffrey himself, by mentioning Avalon as Arthur's resting place, whether from Welsh legend or by a new association of his own invention, had sowed the seeds of the eventual obliteration of the so-called 'Breton hope'. For, some fifty years later, Avalon and Arthur were identified and his grave opened to the world – or so the monks of Glastonbury claimed.

The fullest account of the discovery of this grave, which took place in 1190 or 1191 is given by Giraldus Cambrensis two years later and is worth quoting in full:

Arthur, the famous British king, is still remembered, nor will this memory die out, for he is much praised in the history of the excellent monastery of Glastonbury, of which he himself was in his time a distinguished patron and a generous endower and supporter. . . . His body, for which popular stories have invented a fantastic ending, saying that it had been carried to a remote place, and was not subject to death, was found in recent times at Glastonbury between two stone pyramids standing in the burial ground. It was deep in the earth, enclosed in a hollow oak, and the discovery was accompanied by wonderful and almost miraculous signs. It was reverently transferred to the church and placed in a marble tomb. And a leaden cross was found laid under a stone, not above, as is the custom today, but rather fastened on beneath it. We say this, and traced the inscription which was not showing, but turned in towards the stone: 'Here lies buried the famous king Arthur[2] with Guinevere[3] his second wife in the isle of Avalon.'[4] In this there are several remarkable things: he had two wives, of which the last was buried at the same time as him, and indeed her bones were discovered with those of her husband; how-ever, they were separate, since two parts of the coffin, at the head, were divided off, to contain the bones of a man, while the remaining third at the foot contained the bones of a woman set apart. There was also un-covered a golden tress of hair that had belonged to a beautiful woman, in its pristine condition and colour, which, when a certain monk eagerly snatched it up, suddenly dissolved into dust. Signs that the body had been buried here were found in the records of the place, in the letters inscribed on the pyramids, although these were almost obliterated by age, and in the visions and revelations seen by holy men and clerks; but chiefly through Henry II, King of England, who had heard from an aged British singer that his [Arthur's] body would be found at least sixteen feet deep in the earth, not in a stone tomb, but in a hollow oak. This Henry had told the monks; and the body was at the depth stated and almost concealed, lest, in the event of the Saxons occupying the island, against whom he had fought with so much energy in his lifetime, it should be brought to light, and for that reason, the inscription on the cross which would have revealed the truth, was turned inwards to the stone, to conceal at that time what the coffin contained, and yet inform other centuries. What is now called Glastonbury was in former times called the Isle of Avalon, for it is almost an island, being entirely surrounded by marshes, whence it is named in British Inis Avallon, that is the apple-bearing island, because apples (in British, *aval*) used to abound in that place. Whence Morgan, a noblewoman who was ruler of that region and closely related to Arthur, after the Battle of Camlan carried him away to the island now called Glastonbury to be healed of his wounds. It used also to be called in British Inis Gutrin, that is, the isle of glass; hence the Saxons called it Glastingeburi. For in their tongue glas means glass, and a camp or town is called buri. We know that the bones of Arthur's body that were discovered were so large that in this we might see the fulfilment of the poet's words:

Grandisque effossis mirabitur ossa sepulchris.
[When the graves are opened, they shall marvel at the great size of the bones. (Virgil, *Georgics I*, 497)]

The thigh bone, when placed next to the tallest man present, as the abbot showed us, and fastened to the ground by his foot, reached three inches above his knee. And the skull was of a great, indeed prodigious, capacity, to the extent that the space between the brows and between the eyes was a palm's breadth. But in the skull there were ten or more wounds, which had all healed into scars with the exception of one, which made a great cleft, and seemed to have been the sole cause of death.

His account is confirmed in outline by Ralph of Coggeshall in his *English Chronicle* some thirty years later:

1191: This year were found at Glastonbury the bones of the most renowned Arthur, formerly King of Britain, buried in a very ancient coffin, over which two stone pyramids had been built: on the sides of these was an inscription, illegible on account of the rudeness of the script and its worn condition. The bones were discovered as follows: as they were digging up this ground to bury a monk who had urgently desired in his lifetime to be interred there, they discovered a certain coffin, on which a leaden cross had been placed, bearing the inscription, 'Here lies the famous king Arthur, buried in the isle of Avalon.' For this place, which is surrounded by marshes, was formerly called the isle of Avalon, that is, the isle of apples.

But there is between the two versions an important discrepancy which leads us to question the authenticity of the discovery. Giraldus Cambrensis quotes the words on the cross as '*Hic iacet sepultus inclytus rex Arthurus cum Wenneveria uxore sua secunda in insula Avallonia*'. He repeats it in the *Speculum Ecclesiae* (*Mirror of the Church*) twenty-five years later as: '*Hic iacet sepultus inclytus rex Arthurius in isula Avallonia cum uxore sua secunda Wenneveria.*'[5] But Ralph of Coggeshall, although possibly relying on hearsay, while Giraldus had seen the cross himself, quotes words that agree more closely with later writers: '*Hic iacet inclitus rex Arturius, in insula Avallonis sepultus*'. Leland, in the early sixteenth century, gives: '*Hic*

iacet sepultus inclitus rex Arturius in insula Avalonia' from a copy of the original. He also gives from another source, claiming to be an eyewitness description by one Simon of Abingdon, the very different '*Hic iacet gloriosissimus rex Britonum Arturus*'. Finally, Camden, from whose *Britannia* in the 1610 edition the illustration of the cross is taken, agrees with Leland and Ralph of Coggeshall: '*Hic iacet sepultus inclitus rex Arturius in insula Avalonia.*'

What are we to make of this confusion? There is little doubt that Leland and Camden are quoting accurately what they saw on the copy of the cross which still existed in their day. Camden says of his illustration, '... which inscription or epitaph, as it was sometime exemplified and drawn out of the first copie in the Abbey of Glascon, I thought good for the antiquitie of the characters here to put downe. The letters being made after a barbarous maner, and resembling the Gothish Character, bewray plainly the barbarism of that age. . .'.

It is clearly stated that the cross in Glastonbury Abbey is the 'first copie'. If he means by this the original cross, then our earliest witness is strangely inaccurate; it is far more probable that this is a second version, in which case deliberate alterations have been made. The lettering presents particular problems. It is not unlike ninth-century inscriptions in style; but why should the cross have been made in that period? It seems more likely that someone deliberately worked from an old source; and this could be either the thirteenth-century monks or Camden's informant.[6] If either assumption be correct, the disinterment was staged by the Glastonbury monks.

When we turn to the other aspects of the question, this suspicion is confirmed. There is confusion over the dating: Giraldus Cambrensis in his first account gives no actual year; but in his second, he says that it was in the reign of Henry II, which ended in July 1189, and in the abbacy of Henry of Sully, appointed in the following autumn! Ralph of Coggeshall puts it in 1191, two years later; although the news would scarcely have travelled so slowly as this, a year earlier might be possible without directly contradicting his evidence. Adam of Domerham gives it as 648 years after Arthur's death, which, if he followed Geoffrey of Monmouth's date for the battle of Camlan, would be 1190. This is a peculiar lack of consistency over a recent date, even though medieval chronicles are never exceptionally accurate.

A large number of forgeries of charters and other documents, as well as the interpolations in William of Malmesbury's De Antiquitate Glastoniae, which are now generally recognised as such, but which have long confused the issue, date from this decade onwards. The interpolations, which apparently make the claim that Arthur was buried at Glastonbury before the exhumation of 1190 confirmed it are now dated at about 1250. As to the details of the actual digging, Adam of Domerham, writing the Abbey history a century later, with access to Abbey records, may have unintentionally given us the final clue as to the true nature of the incident when he says that on the day the work began, the spot was surrounded by curtains on the abbot's orders.

An interesting possibility is raised by the mention of a 'hollow oak' in Giruldus' account. It may be that in digging a new tomb in the cemetery, a genuine primitive burial of the dug-out type was discovered. Dug-out burials are described by C. F. C. Hawkes as follows:

> The earlier Northern Bronze Age, indeed, shows the beginning of more than one new departure in the cult of the dead. . . . The bodies were probably deposited . . . in tree-trunk coffins, and inhumation . . . in such coffins was already starting to be practised in Schleswig-Holstein in the beginnings of its Bronze Age. . . . The same rite of boat- or coffin-burial appears simultaneously in Britain in the middle centuries of the second millennium, when the North Sea trade-route was flourishing as already described, penetrating Wessex culture along the south coast, where the burial at Hove . . . was of this type, but more prominent on the east coast, especially in Yorkshire, where the Irish route over the Pennines reached the sea. The classic example is the Gristhorpe coffin-burial near Scarborough, but the recent discovery in the great barrow of Loose Howe on the Cleveland Moors of a primary burial with no less than three boat dug-outs must henceforward stand at the head of the series, and serve to show how the same rite took hold among the seafarers on both sides of the North Sea between about 1600 and 1400 BC.

The actual site of the 'burial' was apparently revealed by excavations in 1962, though the results of these do not seem to have been published in full; it would be almost impossible to determine whether the 'disturbance' then found related to the removal of a particular type of burial. But Glastonbury's past almost certainly included a period as a pagan sanctuary, with which such a hollowed oak burial might have been associated, particularly as the nearby lake village seems to have been an important trading centre.

Nor is a good motive for such a forgery lacking. Arthur's grave was an obvious attraction for pilgrims, and pilgrims were the abbey's chief source of income apart from its properties. They were the only way by which large additional sums could be made; and there was need of extra funds. In 1184, the buildings had been largely burnt down; but Henry II had provided the money for reconstruction. However, when he died in 1189 and Richard came to the throne, the Exchequer's resources were directed entirely to the fitting-out of the Crusade, and the supply of funds ceased. It is strange that within a few months of this, a new source of revenue should suddenly appear. Politically too, it would suit Richard; for the hope of Arthur's return could be used to foment rebellion in Wales, and this discovery seemed to dispose of it. Giraldus tells us that Henry told the monks something about Arthur being buried at Glastonbury; this may be an oblique reference to a hint from Henry that such a discovery would be an acceptable return for his patronage.

Any discussion of the Glastonbury burial will inevitably – like discussion of the historical Arthur – end without definite conclusions being reached. But the circumstantial evidence seems strong enough for us to say that there is not much doubt that the coffin and its contents, or at least its connection with Arthur, were produced by the monks in order to raise the money for the rebuilding of the Abbey, which, forgery or no forgery it certainly did. Nor need all medieval monks be regarded as better in this respect than their secular contemporaries.

The last argument in favour of the interpretation set out above is the persistence of the 'Breton hope' in its original form for another century or more, even after the influence of the Glastonbury story had led to alterations in the romances. William of Rennes, to whom a *Gesta Regum Britanniae* (*Deeds of the Kings of Britain*) of about 1250 is attributed, mentions the tradition as though it were still current. Robert of Gloucester, in about 1290, prefers the Glastonbury story, but leaves little doubt that the other version still had its adherents. Some ten years later Peter Langtoft takes a neutral view, saying he is not sure whether Arthur still lives or not. Robert Mannyng of Brunne calls it the 'Breton lye' writing in 1338. Our last trace of it is in Jehan de Wavrin's chronicle of about 1400, where it seems to be a dead tradition. Surely, if Glastonbury's Arthur were genuine, the old

XVI Illustrations from a three-volumed version of *Lancelot du Lac*, produced in north-eastern France in about 1300.

Lancelot, carrying a white shield, carries off Brandus, Lord of the Dolorous Garde, and is challenged by Sir Keu, who claims the right to take Brandus to King Arthur. They fight and Sir Keu is left wounded. Arthur and his knight ride to where Sir Keu is lying, while Lancelot, bearing his prisoner, gallops into the wood.

The war with Galeholt. Guinevere, the Lady of Malohaut and three attendants survey the battlefield. Lancelot approaches, awaiting a message from the Queen. On the right, Lancelot unhorses Galeholt with a lance given to him by Gawain.

woult la dame de malohaut acc
aiure. Et leua la teste quelle
noir embzunchiac. Et cil uentedi
auront. ear maitre sou lauoit
oie. Et il la regzdat sila come
siebut ceil doloz z ceil anguisi

dautrezldeu bieau donc arrise
auquer puet la moz don cuer ne
ne me puet ullir. Cesti li moz q
prendome me fera de le sui me
longue ment sle auquel puis
ne su ali gair meichi er que de

est ce que uoi auez. aurr. Ha da
me sj dien mei sfaut maut ducy
nulle dller na mon cuer. ec na
mettr saut la bonne voz ne me
poez rauiz embler. ear za uent
maiter choru auceler. Et ie quoy

ullou cuer que jl ne puoie respon
dit ace que la bonne disiue si qui
ea almipurer uult durement
z lez lermez h coule ne coureuall
lez uoez. Si que li saunc quil auo
te uetit euth tout moulloez. Et q
plus reygzdoit la dame de mallo
haut z plus estoit am alause.

ceil moz ne me souuenu. eoh m
moz ma confesse euront mez a
mut esti maz ma con uri maiu
garui. elh moz. ma comr anuz
ear oublier. elh moz ma sagule
enaures mer sauiz. olh maz ua
saut siche enaures mer poure
rez. Par soj saut la sonne euh uaz

bien bie cuer. qui elt la plur il
neit ei. Et ce duc seir elle poz uoir
quelle le puet mettre amalaue
eir elle endort bien sauoir qil
ne peuint damez se ill uon
zamar cuil. jl saut su qlo uener
anz nouer armes. Mais elle
deliuroie eusa malice leour. Tel

III Lancelot, Galeholt and Guinevere are seated on a bench. Galeholt encourages the Queen to kiss Lancelot.
     Under three trees, the seneschal converses with the Lady of Malohaut and another noblewoman.

IV Gawain arrives at the tent of a beautiful damsel, beloved by Hector, and hears their story from her uncle
     the dwarf Groadan.

---

dame. et lou euatr auuz. repi
et tout euglaur z coz jl auoit le
cheual serur. Et jl saut uesti au
reew. que par y pan que jl ue d
uez. Si nere le uau par lez teplez
le siez. et une estache dou pauillo
Et li naual qmenee azuer z dut
oh mott auuiut ce quma mere
me dilinu. Et que sia saut me
sire. Et certer elle ne dut que
malaaue nule mocruit. derces
saut aurures rau moz eteog uaz
ge uos ne me dute qui ea elboir
qui ea elboir qui ploroit z riorí
sur la fontaine. z Pan vos le bai
tutez. Et ten amenuauer ruz deseu
te. Et te duzy saut sl par amet
que tu te gbau ras allu. Et me
sires. dut que tu fi grit auaitage
qui allou suit le gbate. Et puis
qul elt neuuz dea oltir il le con
baron auauz quil ue sache te sl
araunt chacie. Et il enaunte au qi
uan ce quil h demand.

ze dieu saut u uait ce siru

tur. Si ne muiona qire. ear jl na
noit plur de siures que moz. Et
que te su la bonne baila ceste

---

damoiselle la quil nauoit plus
de cou ensuis. Si me gmada sieb
que te lauoie eut que te la grau
siaufle. aussi gme u serue mi en
siur. Et me saut de toute sa vie
q jl reuoiz. qui mir eltoit belle
z riche. mer sieve sila maisena

---

gzo bui lainoiu. ei le ll uguer
bacheler. Et laudauur ma dame
Plui fleui. eil de sa vie qui mir ue
tilleur quelle le preut ear elle eu

oz seune. z pere zde uouez. ei gz
dur par ae ze sauz auit eile. ii
ze eula gzir. que cula silou que
eula gzie le soj vertu. dui sanue
elle ea. Et manute sunt lili lou
quelle le preut. oz m elle pel ue
ne onquer samen. elle onquer uett

Gawain and the daughter of the King of Norgales. He enters the anteroom of her bedchamber, in which twenty knights keep guard: four are shown asleep in their full armour. By the couch is a tall candlestick with a lighted taper, which Gawain is about to put out with an extinguisher. On the right, he kisses the lady, who is lying naked in bed.

Lancelot's madness. Guinevere has hung around Lancelot's neck the shield sent to her by the Lady of the Lake. Lancelot regains his senses and recognises the Queen and the Lady of Malohaut. On the right, the Lady of the Lake, having divined his condition, arrives and anoints Lancelot with unguent, so that he sleeps and recovers.

men lespee emou fiere · et pur
son glaiue qui estoit entre toi
cutes · et uint alon cheual fi
monte · et fapareille deouter
et lau relance dure li aurre che
uall? z il nel luy · si fentr fierent
li durente des glaiues qui unt

don paing de lespee gis cops ou
vi · z on troue · si que maistre mal
les lentout entiees deuar la char
et il a tos iey si plant de cuue qui
nouoit goute · et bn fert que tu
defende unaur cui · si tire a lant ·
mieus et il dit qul fauta aurel uiel

il ne chaut de came · car bn
ne sy puet couser ne gar met
lance euft que il auoit far de
fait de cestuy enla fin de cose
auoit enla cot li chli qui un
tonent · et la some uint alon
raur est iue que plus ne puer

fureut fous aller uolent empie
des · et li chli · dla damoiselle re
ve lui les arcons deluer acerre
auf entudist · dou dur euesecro
quil eur eur · Mais uime gauge

que de son compaignon · elle fieri
de lespee si que toute la teste lefur
Puis remoue fue son cheual ili esl
garde euhaur que sen cheualt a uoir
seus le seneschal · se li dit fous en

liee elle mesmes don homme
banse uoair cous z dit · pur
que beneoir que vos suibes
me li plus preudon don me
uoi effer li chli on mond e

VII   Lancelot fights with three companions of the false Guinevere: two are slain and he is engaging the third. O
       the right, the false Guinevere and the old knight Bertolais are bound to a stake and burnt.

VIII   Lancelot enters the valley of False Lovers. He is attacked by two dragons, but overcomes them and arriv
       at a river to be crossed only by a narrow plank. The way is barred by three knights: the first he throws into t
       river, the other two disappear by enchantment, as do the river and the plank when he uses the ring given to hi
       by the Lady of the Lake. He passes through a wall of fire and comes to steps defended by two knights. He woun
       the first, so that he falls into the flames, the second fares likewise.

longr lctcur don cors uint cou
li bras est tous · et amis le uie
glaiue detous iauute · et que
il uoir quil glaiues au chli
bure a ton escu · a la pure de
ta planche au plus quil puet

cele par lariens que vos plus
anies dureronroi ou eift chli
sont alle ce vous le sanes · et
elle dit que elle nel fer te
diex li dit · Luas est mis ures
de ce quil li sunt eschape · Sua

mer sa maniele · et prent son
escur qui enui la plor de guror
Mas ua auant tant quil uint
a y grant feu qui enui la
uoie estour cell; feus estour si
grans par cimblant truitie

il toute lescur en toure le glai
ue uint quil test bien embru
wes · lors guenehut hors ler
eur de la voie quil ne li uindi
z le lance cheon · en tuane et
tos anus uist bien fon pain

grant piece peur mort en el
rane · et ta damoiselle li demade
quil acenr · ie arendon fint il
celuy · couars maudais qui
sen tout fous · que ie doure ili
ne reuaingueur ia quil te me

riens ni entrar qui ne fhu
ro · et durut don mia a det
minia celui il feucur · prar
d'ais cel feu auoir par degre
qui mouteoir en une cate ou
des feus estoir int bele · mais
ti aegre

x Karadoc, an evil knight of great strength, has captured Gawain, and put him in the Dolorous Tower. Lancelot attacks Karadoc by raising his sword: it will be shivered on the steps, but a maiden stands above, holding out a sword fated to provide Karadoc's death. Karadoc knew this, but entrusted the sword to the maiden, believing her to be true to him. Within the battlemented wall of the Tower, Lancelot throws the headless Karadoc into a pit, while Gawain escapes from his prison.

x Lancelot, in disguise, undergoes the disgrace of being drawn in a cart by a dwarf on horseback. The dwarf has promised Lancelot that if he submits, he will take him within sight of Guinevere, who has been captured by Meleagant, son of King Baudemagus of Gorre. They approach the castle, followed by Gawain and two squires. Gawain is also in search of the Queen and does not recognise Lancelot, because, according to the conventions of knighthood, Lancelot would never allow himself to be driven in such a shameful way.

l preudon le maine acelle
tombe · Et une lame gn
sont sur de marbre · qui bie auoit
iii · pies · dle · par aual · Z uis g
amour · z bien auoit delper un
grant pie · et estoir suelsee a
plonc · Za ciment · Uees · ci les
say sur li preudan · qui ceste la
me porta leuer par son cors sla
cheualerie lauentur que h gret

guement tant lance · la lame de
sour du chies · Et qui si la uoit
mettre sus a le rine enlau · eus g
me il lauoir leuee conquer pe
ne uauala sus · De ceste chose
fure ur esbahi trop durement
z un sautre · Et li preudo dist
a lame · sire ceste auenture aue
uous acomplie · Et ie ne crouis
iamais enchose qui doie auenir

ua · Et lance · auale les degres con
troual la caue · Et uoit tres suu
la caue une grit lame · et are m
angunsenblement · descouert part p
la flame enuoie contremont duuale
haut que une lance · z maine tel
bruit z cest noise · quand on mdle
a hardi qui non soit auoir pas
il resgarde la lame longuement
qui maine grant dole · il le uent

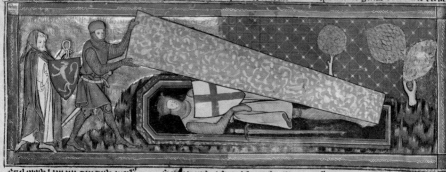

Et il meist lamain tantost aupr
gros chies · Et rivulthe il dure
ment quil uour la nourur dou

ce por vous ne sont deliure li euil
lie · Atant le maistuer au moustier
z rendu gracie a nostre signor

Ptat · Dee qui estoir venu · en il
nenoir une guene si pront lama
nestre que tout nestoit dre state

pour · Et ie leu voe uedoir laus
mable ce que voe eites venu; dre
lauerie; plus ligerement · Et ne
vorroie bn te cathie; car veiter
hous ou monde por eu ie serrie
ur · Por mos biau dire sur lame

eu bar sane our il roit alane · qui
eit mouces; Atan vout grit aleur
eula eure sile sur li soit entrer en
la plus celee chambre qui soit leaug
Atra reine; Abec lui z toute gent
que i seul estonir qui fera ce que

honos certer sur est te non inoi
pour · ancou seront grit conardie
Atus bien que voe eiter faillie
euer · ou voe doutre; celui ou voue
me hae; qui ceme dme; auisen e
mas hautt · sle la see se ceste laus

auge pas voe itrie; tant · car
me sui ouquer de vous acourte ve
ne se u ne vousui ouques
mien endiere; ajar ques; que ie
se siners mos ma bataille auons

li gnanden · Et le gard il un met
serrer leaus · pee que descouu
nele voelr une couretier Apres
est li soit venui alon bd · z li dut
Biaus her tuar veut maille bel

ge me esportce; car iai alle zeu
er · z soie dn acendre · z a obaf
gtre lui · Et le vos laue; liberghe
contre mos tant auenuge pr grit
honos; enina droiture dessendre

el parm la rouge men
... pharauz; les sueur por
... ? eu; me eruue me oduir
... ques; me mestre; veliu sau
... rualus. Je su sauir josep un;
... res. Eu wes sauir eu. Zvellu bu
... el garu. Ohl mir bien sauir

... reces; Seu rouge li mauger demat
... ralaur. ? respondi mesir aures; ol
... est ce sauc si en qui les ymages
... corruues eroz que les gens
... our sauir delor mains; eroy que
... ce souenr dieu. ? que il au or pl

... auoir rire graus; ? belles eel
... chaltaus; su mlt biau; ? mour
... soz; ? mlt riches; ? auoir auoy
... la rothe. Si eroir eloc d' bon
... mur rout eroz; ? d' fode; gso ?
... parsonz; ? estuir rrop bien au

josep. Dour enuenureu a
moj sauir li sariatuus. en une
... e ere auaur. eur uus mes;
... es eue maladez plus a dun
... dune plane quil a evla reue
... poure neudeuz le peur. Si uou
... sauir josep. Si me Were eui

... puissance soz; eoz que tu soz auy.
... Ohl sauir li sariatuus wedis que
... les ymage sour puissaur. non
... par s; les ymages obaue s; era u
... en eui non les ymages sor sauree;
... ? dour euer our sublaues. Zeu
... eui non wes les euereuouz. Eur
... uour sauour auneuour aue

... siez; de route chose que abon
... chatel guenoir. Oliss josep. Su
... entres; ou chatel a Wee le eura
... siu. Si euconrre eur p. lyon;
... rour d'ethaue qui ethapes er
... ? d'auoir parmi la mauure
... rue. Et la ou il vir le thir ar
... mes Si li couru auu; Je sauf par

III Gawain and nine companions rescue a knight being attacked by ten others. The knight carries two swords
and explains that one of them was used by a Saracen to kill Joseph of Arimathea. The sword broke, leaving one
piece in Joseph's body, and it was foretold that the two parts would be reunited by the man destined to
accomplish the high adventures of the Holy Grail, and no other. Gawain tries, but sorrowfully fails, as do all his
companions. They go in search of Lancelot.

IV Gawain and Hector enter a cemetery, despite a warning inscription on a tomb at the entrance. They see a
tomb from which flames leap up to the height of a lance, surrounded by an upright sword. Gawain enters first, but
cannot reach the burning tomb because swords rise up of their own accord and strike him. He retires and Hector
is depicted falling on one knee, receiving five swords on his shield and helmet.

... gaunaueueur. eur mlt ai grat
... ng uille aucuer. sle we we evp; i
... me douue ouqueri maz aueaur
... ue ve sar oz euduor. Z si aj duel

... peue; ce rou riju rrop erbauy;
... qui mlt uem poouer sauir.
... eur rrop estueur laue; z eauuu
... Si que apauue pooeur il we

... ou il auoir uue cov; d'euz; z a
... eue eroz; auoir lerruez eereprer
... Gau disteur. Oru. thir; cree
... paruuz; qui ea chemmes Vou

... au re parr. eur ue siz li plu;
... riche auz chis; dou moude. qu
... lue estre li miey cheauz; draiz
... re sauir herdez. encore uest pac
... Si hebu; aau il we vor mehe
... en aneuue chose aueuue foz
... poure neudeuz uour par ev
... d' eorreez. Por uour heer

... leruey auuru y eheues d' piece
... S drean, hee. eu estauz. ? reulgar
... da euuuy lu auu que si eur
... dormy. Z rrou a uue rerra qui
... disteur. jamau uuz; chis; nou
... uel adour dour lu sul ala sonue
... dole rouse juenu. ? wes lesmor

... au; voue; sue adelte ? lauuy
... asseurure. Gar delrier que
... tu ar leruey ? ta veue. que eu
... eui adelre auueure wee mor
... tez d' eeus adelre we digge me
... eur si mal par la gso peril eue
... ila euelle asseurure. eur uu;
... sle sempur parriz sauf hou

Rmiator. Li on vous covez
le Roi artus. amoy escriex er
ma dame la Roine. Pour tel ca
mere. ambe dus & par moy. Si
procureres ama dame lecha
quier. z tes eschas. z les dire tou
la manere. z la fort draus.

le Rur. z il dut mlt bien dieu ni
er. car il na encore ganer que te
leu lun z baute. Los araint tel
eschac. z leschaquier qui estoit
en y forel & thes Si la genoille
auant la Roine. z dist. Nme la
celuz don lac vous en voie cest er

eur par vaus encontr la Roine
z il le crement a retbancement
z enchantemens tanz finne qui
estr ta Roine et paine & bes
merspee que maine hart baro
restoient venur posh resgant
Maz onquet il bien qes gard

er counce: y mient ie ler a gad
guies. z il dut que cest messagr
fera il bien. Los prent lecha
quier z tes eschas z ses cheual
z il pare d'eaus. z escrit tant pur
se consees. quil unt akamal
las. er bien tes laina auchas

chas. par conent que vous ne
veutes onquet iour & vre. vne
aussi muleus. ne si bieber ne
poes vous auoir veuz. Que la
Roine oit cel nouuelles. Si entla
a muuelles ba. Si Rur acanou
le nam a une mus. 2h mut

que elle ne puit matre entana
er lors ymence la rise pur le
palaz. & ce que la Roine a vega
perdue. Et li Rad mesines lina
guibaur z la Roine d'manda
elu. de lanc messinez ynouu
nes z il dut a vne autar amo

XV   Lancelot ends the enchantment of the Lost Forest and a magic chessboard is brought to him. The piece
of gold and silver, move of their own accord and hitherto nobody has won a game. Lancelot plays and wins, so th
chessboard is declared his. He sends it as a gift to Guinevere, who is shown sitting with King Arthur. She pla
her best, but loses.

XVI   The Tourney at Camelot. Lancelot has been maligned by certain knights of the Round Table. He receives
message from Guinevere to take the side of King Baudemagus. Bearing a red shield so that nobody shoul
recognise him, Lancelot overthrows all his opponents until he comes to the Queen, watching the tourney with he
ladies. At the sight of the Queen, he falls into a swoon, and has to be rescued and carried into a wood b
Baudemagus. Here he sleeps and recovers.

flu onquet ame von tat one net
au matte thir dou mode. de Pur
la motne & proece que est almi
cur par so cors. Car il ne fina bun
& ferir ne puis ne recerar neque

qui pue voir que vous ne res:
ne: plus voures acer. Et la Roine
qui bn oit cel paroles: z se resgnt
z qui voir auder celui cui elle
mandent rir. Si resgn tesi ami

cheoir a y mient. Si na qune
rreigne Si resgnz & ver luy
voir le Roi baudmagus Gh dut
Sur z dieu reue: moi ent sug
bna. car vos me vez. ia cheoir

de fut une auermis. Que li Ros
oit cette nouuelle. Si nest mie pe
gir eschabis. Car mlt li annera
ill voir sigrur guerpu la place
& poour aler a cmis. Los egrere
lanc. z dut mlt dolant: z mlt cour
cies. Pai lanc biaus dour ami.
Oz vogr bn qer est ma marson

qui voir z vie ur aussi ligrerent
pu tant. yme si vemi ame &
nant luy. z voir yme le fuent
aussi yme ill veister la maz ve
mir. z plarst alec ferai z eschatr
duant les autres. don estonent
thescuans qui accurent ne voleur
quil est venu: z vait les logre

atre: se il nai aub. Car se me fer
si matade or endroit que ie en
bn morir encestre place. Que tu
vous oit cette pole. Sa pale qui
ne sur nauree: amor elle pep
entr des bras mlt doucement
z quidee alarr th grant duel:
li smdan. Pai sir dieu etter li
nauret adur le voil madiaie

stories which gave quite different accounts of his end would not have taken two hundred years to die.

It is possible that another reason for choosing to 'discover' Arthur was that Glastonbury had already been equated with Avalon. In 1136 it was known to the Welsh as Inis Gutrin (Isle of Glass). And among the Welsh other-worlds was an Isle of Glass, which appears in the poem *The Spoils of Annwfn*, already mentioned. Its climate, like that of Avalon in the *Life of Merlin*, was remarkably mild. Both Glastonbury and this Isle of Glass were associated with Melwas. There were connections enough to enable Glastonbury to be identified as Avalon.

Even after 1400, belief in Arthur's return still recurs. But it has passed into the realms of folklore; some stories describe him as wandering in the form of a bird, usually a Cornish chough, or a raven. Most of these tales conform to a definite type, that of the sleeping warrior who will one day reappear as leader when called by the breaking of a spell. Such stories have been told of every great national hero, and are readily adaptable to new names and characters as events provide them. The earliest appearance of Arthur in this role is recorded in Gervase of Tilbury's *Otia Imperialia* (*Imperial Trifles*) (after 1214). The writer knows the current Avalon version, but also describes the recent adventure of the groom of an Italian bishop, who, while following a stray horse on Mount Etna, came across Arthur in a sort of Earthly Paradise, entered by a cleft in the rock. There are other similar stories of Arthur and Etna of this period explained by the Norman presence in Sicily.

In Britain, there are two important versions of the story, the best known being attached to Craig-y-Dinas near Snowdon and some other Welsh caves.[7] On London Bridge, a Welshman with a hazel staff meets a stranger who tells him that a treasure lies hidden under the tree from which the staff was cut. They return together to Wales, and find the tree, and a cave beneath it. In the passage leading to the cave hangs a bell which must on no account be touched. If it rings, the warriors in the cave, among whom is Arthur, waiting to lead the Welsh to their former glory, will awake and ask, 'Is it day?' The answer must be, 'No, sleep thou on.' This happens: but the correct answer is given, and the Welshman is able to take some of the treasure. On his next visit he forgets the formula, and is beaten until he is crippled by the warriors. He is never able to find the cave again.

The other version is found at Sewingshields on the Roman wall, and at Richmond in Yorkshire. The visitor finds Arthur, Guinevere and his Court sleeping by a table on which lie a garter, a sword and a bugle. The garter must be cut and the horn blown, at which Arthur will arise and lead the Britons to victory. But the visitor only does the first and Arthur wakes only to fall asleep again. The Richmond version concerns one Potter Thompson, who is dismissed with these words by Arthur:

> Potter Thompson, Potter Thompson, hadst thou blown the horn,
> Thou hadst been the greatest man that ever was born.

A similar rhyme is used at Sewingshields. Other northern localities have similar stories; as with the Welsh legend, the place-name was changed by each storyteller.

Cadbury in Somerset also claims to be Arthur's sleeping-place, although he has never been seen there. It was here in about 1880 that the incident told by Deran Robinson took place. A visiting party of antiquaries were asked by an old man living nearby whether they had 'come to take away the king'. This tradition, however, goes back to a sixteenth-century identification of Cadbury with Camelot, first recorded by Leland:

> At the very south ende of the chirch of South-Cadbyri standith Camallate, sumtyme a famose toun or catelle, apon a very torre or hille, wunderfully enstrengtheid of nature. . . . In the upper parte of the coppe of the hille be 4. diches or trenches, and a balky waulle of yerth betwixt every one of them. In the very toppe of the hille above al the trenchis is *magna area* or *campus* of a 20. acres or more by estimation, wher yn dyverse places men may se fundations and *rudera* of walles. There was much dusky blew stone that people of the villages therby hath caryid away. . . . Much gold, sylver and coper of the Romaine coynes hath be found ther yn plouing; and lykewise in the rootes of this hille, with many other antique thinges, and especial by este. Ther was found *in hominum memoria* a horse shoe of sylver at Camallate.
> The people can telle nothing ther but that they have hard say that Arture

66

much resortid to Camalat. ... Diverse villages there about bere the name Camalat by an addition, as Quene-Camallat, and other.

Leland betrays the reason for the original association of Cadbury and Camelot: the fortuitous presence nearby of a village named Camel, from the early form Cantmael found as far back as the tenth century. 'Queen's' refers to Edward I's gift of it to his wife in 1284. And we have already seen how slight the possible archaeological links between Arthur and Cadbury camp are; this is no echo of an old tradition, but the chance identification of two similar names.

5

The Matter of Britain: Romances in French

Arthur reached his greatest fame in a world far removed from his Celtic origins, and when we think of him today it is usually in the character given him by twelfth- and thirteenth-century French romances. We have already touched on the difficult problem of how the Celtic stories which provided these writers with their material, the *matière de Bretagne*[1] or 'matter of Britain' were transplanted across the channel. Our first written tale dates from the middle of the twelfth century, though there are short poems, known as the Breton *lais*, which may be earlier contain single episodes from Arthurian stories. So it seems probable that there was a period when the Arthurian stories were recited before they came to be recorded in writing; and we can only make tentative reconstruction of their content in this 'oral' stage. The Breton *lais* do offer one possible hint. Most of their plots derive from well-known folklore themes. Their characterisations of the figures of Arthur's Court are fairly simple; for example, in *Lanval*, Arthur's unnamed queen tries to seduce the hero, foreshadowing Guinevere's adultery in later romance. But could not this also be the intermediate stage from which longer stories developed? By combining a number of such episodes within a broader framework of Arthur's Court as depicted by Geoffrey and his followers, and filling out the characters, we would arrive at something not unlike the work of Chrétien de Troyes or the authors of the *Mabinogion* romances. Where and how the work of composition took place we cannot tell, and there is no particular reason to prefer France, Brittany or Wales.

The first fully-developed romance seems to have been a *Tristan* of about 1150, but it is Chrétien de Troyes, who began to write soon after this, who represents the mainstream of strictly Arthurian literature. Born before 1130, Chrétien was closely associated with the Court of Champagne and particularly with the Countess Marie, daughter of Eleanor of Aquitaine. From her motheer, Marie had inherited a taste for literature, particularly that of the Provençal troubadours; and the ideal of courtly love flourished in her circle. Chrétien's first works seem to have been a translation of Ovid's *Art of Love*, a popular work in the Middle Ages, and a version of the Tristan legend. Both of these are lost, and the *Erec* of about 1170 is his earliest surviving piece. It was followed by the nominally Arthurian *Cligès*, drawn largely from classical legend and using Arthur's Court merely as a backdrop, and the important *Lancelot* (*Le Chevalier de la Charette*), *Yvain* (*Le Chevalier au Lion*), both written about 1179, and *Perceval* (*Le Conte du Graal*). The last was left unfinished, and dates from 1180–90.

Chrétien's handling of *Erec* sets certain patterns which were to endure throughout medieval Arthurian romance. Erec wins Enide as his bride by achieving two quests, perhaps separate stories linked by Chrétien. He then brings her to Arthur's Court, where she is received with great honour; and this affords an opportunity for Chrétien to describe the characters of the Court and its splendours, and to display his own learning in Arthurian matters. The main psychological action follows: how Erec abandons knightly ways for Enide's charms, and, on hearing her reproach herself for this, mistakenly suspects her fidelity. The testing of both Erec's knightly prowess and his wife's faithfulness is worked out in a series of loosely-linked adventures, again drawn from Celtic prototypes and including such themes as an encounter with a dwarf king which recur in many later works. When both Erec and Enide have been proved true, a last section forms the climax: Erec breaks an enchantment by which a king and his Court are bound. It is as though the power to do this had only been established by his previous trials, though Chrétien does not make this explicit. The poem ends with the coronation of Erec and Enide as heirs to his father's kingdom.

The framework, with its three clearly defined divisions, betrays a mind trained in formal literary conventions, and is certainly Chrétien's own device. The actual content of the story is centred on the folklore theme of Patient Griselda, which accounts for the main action; and the details are drawn from the Celtic-French material already described, though only the last exploit, the so-called *Joie de la Cort*, has the characteristic fey quality of such adventures, with half-explained enchantments and disenchantments whose logic is not that of the rational world. The great appeal of this combination to contemporary audiences was its presentation of a familiar world with this fantastic surrounding of adventure. The familiar world is also transformed but only by making everything more splendid and dramatic until it transcends reality. Arthur's Court is like any ordinary Court, but peopled with heroes and bedecked in the richest furnishings; Arthur himself is a king such as every knight dreamed of, generous and a great encourager of prowess, quite untrammelled by everyday considerations.

Chrétien's next romance, *Cligès*, illustrates the way in which quite different stories could be drawn into the Arthurian web simply by using Arthur's Court as a background. On this point, it is interesting that Chrétien, the first so to depict the Round Table as a great centre of chivalry, was also the first to name Arthur's capital Camelot, a name he may have found in *Camulodunum*, the Roman name for Colchester. *Cligès* tells of the love of Alexander and Fenice, and of their son Cligès for Soredamors; much of the action takes place in Constantinople, and lacks the mysterious atmosphere of the other romances; as a result, none of the characters or episodes play an important part in later Arthurian stories.

In *Lancelot*, or as it is more often known, *Le Chevalier de la Charette* (*The Knight of the Cart*), Chrétien introduced for the first time one of the most important elements of the romances: the idea of courtly love. It is important to distinguish between the passionate, unrestrained love of Tristan and Isolt and the carefully restrained code of courtly love. The latter (with which Chrétien does not seem to have altogether sympathised, since he firmly declares that he only wrote the tale at Marie de Champagne's bidding, and left it to another poet to finish) was derived from the literature of southern France, where, from the beginning of the twelfth century, the troubadours had elaborated on the theme of the superiority of the lady and the moral worth to which the worshipping lover could attain, investing the beloved with an aura of divinity which still lingers about Guinevere in Chrétien's tale. Utter obedience was required if the lover was to gain solace, though in the strictest schools such solace was no more than a chaste kiss. Hence Lancelot is rebuked for hesitating a moment in mounting an executioner's cart, when his duty to Guinevere required him to do so after his horse had been slain as he rode to her rescue. Chrétien does not hold to the principle of courtly love with its implied adultery, probably because of the original from which he was working: his own view of love was much more moral, as witness Fenice's proud rejection, in *Cligès*, of Isolt's fate: 'Never could I agree to live the life that Isolt lived; love was debased in her for her body was at the disposal of two, and her heart was wholly for one . . . Let him who has the heart have the body and exclude all others.'

The story of *The Knight of the Cart* is that of Guinevere's abduction by Meleagant (otherwise the Melwas of the *Life of St Gildas*) which appears in Malory's last book. The all-important theme is that of Lancelot as lover and rescuer, whether performing heroic feats, falling into an ecstasy at the sight of his mistress' golden hairs on a comb she has left behind, or playing the coward at a tournament at her command. The adventures are full of marvels and mysteries, of perilous beds and flaming lances; perhaps the most famous is that of the bridge made of a single sharp sword blade which Lancelot has to crawl across in order to reach Guinevere's prison. However much Chrétien may disclaim his responsibility for both subject and moral, he has succeeded in combining all the essential ingredients of Arthurian romance for the first time, quite apart from his own masterly portrait of the lovelorn Lancelot and his distant, divine lady. The weakness of the poem is in the mechanism of the action, which remains unexplained and unmotivated except where the lovers are concerned. A wider canvas was needed in order to give the causes and consequences of the adventures, and the final effect is of a cameo rather than a complete work of art.

Chrétien is obviously more at ease in *Yvain* or *Le Chevalier au Lion* (*The Knight with the Lion*), which may have been written at the same time as *The Knight of the Cart*. Here the theme is a moral one, and harks bark to *Erec*, to which it is in many ways a counterpart. In the first part, Yvain wins and marries Lunete by his prowess, but is lured away to Arthur's Court in search of fame; promising to return in a year and a day, he breaks his pledge, and is rejected by his lady; and the second part describes his adventures in regaining her favour, in which he is assisted by a lion which he has rescued from a serpent. If the theme of the lion comes from the classical story of Androcles, the marvels are again Celtic, particularly the splendid episode of the fountain in the forest of Broceliande:

It must have been after nine o'clock and might have been drawing on toward noon when I espied the tree and the chapel. . . . From the tree I saw the basin hanging, of the finest gold that was ever for sale in any fair. As for the spring, you may take my word that it was boiling like hot water. The stone was of emerald, with holes in it like a cask, and there were four rubies underneath, more radiant and red than is the morning sun when it rises in the east. Now not one word will I say which is not true. I wished to see the marvellous appearing of the tempest and the storm; but therein I was not wise, for I would gladly have repented, if I could, when I had sprinkled the perforated stone with the water from the basin. But I fear I poured too much, for straightway I saw the heavens so break loose that from more than fourteen directions the lightning blinded my eyes, and all at once the clouds let fall snow and rain and hail. The storm was so fierce and terrible that a hundred times I thought I should be killed by the bolts which fell about me and by the trees which were rent apart. . . . As soon as the storm was completely past, I saw so many birds gathered in the pine tree that not a branch or twig was to be seen which was not entirely covered with birds. The tree was all the more lovely then, for all the birds sang in harmony, yet the note of each was different, so that I never heard one singing another's note . . . I stayed there until I heard some knights coming, as I thought – it seemed that there must be ten of them. But all the noise and commotion was made by the approach of a single knight.

Like *Erec*, *Yvain* is a self-contained work and was never integrated into the later romance cycles, though its popularity is witnessed by Welsh and English translations. Though it presents no novelties, it is probably Chrétien's masterpiece, a beautifully coherent and balanced story which uses the adventures as part of the wider pattern of sin committed and forgiveness earned.

Chrétien's last, unfinished work, *Perceval* or *Le Conte du Graal* (*The History of the Grail*) once again points the way forward. The plot, that of a simpleton, who, brought up far from the haunts of men, wins his own way in the world through a series of adventures caused by his ignorance, contained the germs of the development of the whole spiritual element in the Arthurian cycle. What Chrétien himself intended by the Grail we shall never know. Such evidence as there is points to a kind of dish of plenty for which Chrétien chose to use a rare French word *graal* from the late Latin *gradalis*. Such all-providing dishes or cauldrons are fairly frequent in Celtic literature; Arthur himself seizes one from the High Steward of the King of Ireland in *Culhwch and Olwen*. Furthermore, the cauldron was a symbol of spiritual nourishment, the source of poetic inspiration or *awen*, in some Welsh tales, which would suggest more mysterious functions than mere feasting. There are difficulties and inconsistencies in plenty in Chrétien's account, and for once it seems as though the marvels of the Celtic original proved too much for his more rational approach. While he usually makes clear how any given marvel happened, he is never particularly troubled by the why or wherefore. Here, however, the Grail procession, the wounded king and the asking of a ritual question are all interlinked and Chrétien does not seem to be able to explain why this should be so. Perhaps it was difficulties with his material rather than lack of opportunity that led him to leave the tale incomplete, as the following outline may indicate.

Perceval is brought up by his mother in ignorance of chivalry, since his father and elder brothers have been slain while knights-errant. Perceval meets five knights by chance, and deserts his mother to seek knighthood, armed only with hasty advice from her on his conduct (which he misunderstands) and crude home-made equipment. The simpleton's misunderstandings and ignorance lead to his first adventures: he compromises a lady by kissing her against her will, and slays a kinsman for his armour. He even fails to grasp the friendly teaching of Gornemant de Gohort, who tells him that to talk or question too much is ill-mannered. His only success is with the beautiful Blancheflor, whom he rescues from her enemies, though he quits her embraces to seek his mother again, not knowing that she has died of a broken heart.

On his quest, he meets a mysterious fisherman, who offers him shelter in his castle. He rides there, to find his host already reclining on a couch in the great hall. He is given a sword, and the procession of the *graal* then enters: a youth bearing a lance which bleeds from the point, two squires carrying golden candelabra, a beautiful maiden who tends the golden *graal* itself, which is covered in precious stones, and lastly a damsel carrying a silver carving dish. Remembering Gornemant's instructions, Perceval forebears to question his host as to the meaning of this ceremony. The following morning the castle is empty; he learns from a girl whom he meets in the forest that his failure to enquire about the *graal* will be disastrous for the land around.

The remainder of the poem concerns Perceval's adventures in his search for the way back to the castle of the *graal* and Gawain's part in seeking the Bleeding Lance. As the story breaks off, Gawain's mysterious adventures have come to dominate the poem, though Perceval learns from a hermit that the Fisher King is his cousin, and is sustained by a single mass wafer served to him each day in the *graal*.

Chrétien's intention seems to have been to use Gawain as a kind of worldly counterpart to Perceval; what he achieves is an intermingling of themes which later romancers were to adopt as one of their principal methods of construction. And even if Chrétien had completed the work, it is by no means certain that he would have entirely explained his mysteries, since many later writers use this technique of alternating stories to gloss over inconsistencies or to include marvels which are less meaningful than they appear. Some of Chrétien's marvels, so R. S. Loomis has persuasively argued, derive from misreadings of earlier French versions, whose crude renderings made the details of the story incomprehensible. Thus the mass wafer carried in the *graal* may be a misreading of *cors beneit*, a blessed or magical *horn* (of plenty) as the Blessed *Body* (of Our Lord); and elsewhere a man sitting at a silver chessboard becomes a man with a silver leg, while a throne carved with eagles becomes a bundle of rushes!

Furthermore, Chrétien's failure to complete the poem suggested to other writers that a completion might be provided, just as later writers took up unexplained details to build up a cycle of romances running from the Crucifixion to Arthur's death. The continuators took a further thirty to forty thousand lines (in variant versions) to complete Chrétien's work. The first of them concentrated on Gawain, who finds the Grail castle; here we learn that the lance is that which pierced Christ's side at the Crucifixion, an important eloboration of the story. The second writer returns to Perceval, keeping more closely to Chrétien's intentions, and ends with Perceval's unsuccessful return to the Grail castle, where he sees the vessel again, now said to contain Christ's blood, but fails to mend completely a magical sword. The last part by one Manessier, reverts to Chrétien's original Grail procession, but this was only finished in the mid-thirteenth century, by which time new versions of the whole story, complete in themselves, had already appeared.

Chrétien, as we have seen, worked largely on material which he shaped in general outline and content, using details borrowed from Celtic tradition. With the story of Tristan and Isolt the reverse is true: the plot and events remain constant, deriving from Celtic and other, often exotic material, while it is the details which tend to change for each new audience. Marie de France and two of the troubadours mention Tristan as an ideal lover in the 1160s, and Chrétien's claim to have made a version of the legend supports the idea that it was already widely known. The earliest surviving fragments are of a poem by Thomas, who wrote at the Plantagenet Court in England some time after 1150. He was followed by Eilhart von Oberge, working from a different French version into German about 1170, and by another Norman poet, Béroul, about 1190.

The central theme of these romances, the love of Tristan for Isolt, wife of his uncle Mark, is found in Welsh literature and scholars generally accepted that the original Tristan was Drust, son of the Pictish king Talorc who ruled in Scotland about 780, and that the legends were later relocated in Cornwall, as were those about Arthur himself. The so-called Tristan stone at Castledor refers to another character of similar name, and its only connection with the legend is that it may have suggested the new site of the stories. In Welsh legend, Essyllt's lover is always Tristan 'son of Tallwch' and the Cornish Drustanus' father is named in the inscription as Cunomorus. Even so the shape of the legend was drawn by Welsh writers from Irish sources, adding the story of Diarmaid and Grainne to an episode about Drust which told how he rescued a foreign king from having to surrender his daughter as tribute by defeating a hero in single combat. This theme, similar to the story of Theseus in Greek myth, suggested the addition of other details from the Theseus legends: the half-bestial nature of his adversary (as with the Minotaur) and the use of the black and white sails as a signal of failure or success. Other incidents were drawn into the story from sources as far afield as India and Arabia, brought perhaps by travelling merchants; and merchants figure in the poem as the cause of Tristan's arrival in Cornwall from Brittany. The power of the central love-story has attracted all kinds of lesser folklore in which the same triangle of characters is repeated.

The story as given in the original version runs as follows. Tristan is the son of Rivalen and Blancheflor, the sister of King Mark of Cornwall. His father was slain in battle and his mother died in childbirth; hence his name, implying sorrow (*tristesse*). He came incognito to Mark's Court, and soon distinguished himself by knightly feats, in particular by slaying the Irish champion Morholt, who came every seven years to demand a tribute of young men and girls from the Cornish king. Morholt's body was taken back to Ireland, where his niece, the Princess Isolt, removed a piece of Tristan's sword, swearing to use it to trace his slayer and exact vengeance. Tristan came to Ireland in search for a bride for King Mark and won Isolt by slaying a dragon, but he was overcome by the dragon's poison, and a seneschal falsely claimed to have achieved the exploit.

As Isolt tended Tristan's wounds, she noticed the gap in the blade of his sword, but since only he could save her from the seneschal, refrained from killing him when he was unarmed. Tristan duly took her back to Cornwall as his uncle's bride, but on the voyage a magic philtre intended for her wedding night was given to the pair by mistake. Brangain, Isolt's faithful maid, took her place on her wedding night in King Mark's bed; and the lovers yielded to their passion, resorting to all kinds of trickery to deceive King Mark; when Mark, at last convinced of their guilt, made Isolt swear that she was faithful by the ordeal of holding a red-hot iron, she arranged for Tristan to disguise himself as a pilgrim. As she approached the place of the ordeal, she stumbled into his arms, and altered the oath to swear that she had never been touched by any man save her husband and the pilgrim. She survived the ordeal unscathed, but Mark later banished the lovers. Hunting in the forest, he once came across them asleep, with a naked sword between them, which again persuaded him of their innocence. As a precaution, he banished Tristan, who crossed to Brittany and married Isolt of the White Hands, sister of Prince Kaherdin. However, he never consummated the marriage, and when this came to light, persuaded Kaherdin that he meant no insult and offered to show him the Irish Isolt. They travelled in disguise to Cornwall where Kaherdin fell in love with Isolt's maid. They had to return to Brittany, where after a number of adventures, Tristan was wounded by a poisoned arrow. Sending for Isolt of Ireland to heal him, he instructed the messenger to hoist black sails if he returned without her, white sails if his quest was successful. Isolt of Brittany, jealous of the other Isolt, falsely told him that the sails were black at which he died of grief, as did Isolt of Ireland on finding she had arrived too late.

Eilhart and Béroul took this relatively sophisticated story, with its complex sequence of episodes, and did little more than retell it in their own way, making minor alterations but leaving the working of the tragedy of guilty love unchanged. Even though Tristan and Isolt stand in the same relation to Mark as the lover and lady in the stock situation of courtly love to the lord, neither poet takes a 'courtly' attitude towards them. Some of the episodes are of a primitive cruelty, as when Isolt is about to be burnt for adultery and a company of lepers suggest that a more fitting fate would be for her to be given to them as their whore. There are a few psychological elaborations, and the lovers' passion is neither praised nor blamed by either writer. Eilhart sees the love-potion as the one cause of their woe; once they have tasted 'the most unlucky drink', they are doomed. Béroul, on the other hand, apportions no moral blame but sees Mark's conduct towards the lovers in terms of strictly legal rights. Mark refuses Tristran the customary trial by battle and thenceforward is in the wrong, since Tristan is never legally proved guilty; and the episode of the ambiguous oath fits in with this legalistic attitude very well. These two early versions of the legend are more realistic and down to earth than what followed, but the lovers lack fire and character: the mainspring of their actions is scarcely more than physical desire, however fierce or passionate.

With Thomas the emphasis changes considerably. The story is subordinated to the study of feeling, much in the manner of Chrétien's *Cligès*, and from physical realism we move into emotional realism. The crux is therefore the truth of Tristan and Isolt's love: the effect of the love-potion does not abate, as in Eilhart and Béroul, because it is not an external force but a symbol of an internal emotion and Tristan's marriage to Isolt becomes another of the tests of the lovers' fidelity. In similar vein, Thomas introduces the *Salle aux Images* (hall of statues) to which Tristan retreats secretly to worship an image of Isolt of Cornwall, an idea which comes near to the veneration of the troubadours for their ladies. But there is none of the restraining *mezura* ('measure in all things') of the Provencal poets here, no holding back from the physical consummation of spiritual desire. But Thomas does not entirely achieve the glorification of love which he attempts, because he is too respectful of the original version. It was only his German translator, Gottfried von Strassburg, who realised the full possibility of the story.

Thomas entirely excludes Arthur from his poem, making Mark King of England, and the Tristan legend only returned to the Arthurian fold in the next century. Elsewhere, however, Arthur's fictional kingdom continued to grow. Soon after the early continuations of

Chrétien's *Perceval*, work began on a group of poems which were to develop into a complete cycle of prose stories on Arthur's career from birth to death, known to scholars as the Vulgate Cycle. The forerunner of this massive compilation was a similar series beginning with the early history of the Grail. Robert de Boron, though we know little about him, seems to have written about 1200; and his work, as it survives (*Joseph d'Arimathie* and a fragment of *Merlin*) poses so many questions that we can only touch on them briefly here. The biggest difficulty is that within two decades of the appearance of the enigmatic *graal* in Chrétien's work, Robert offers a complete and circumstantial history of it, equating it with the Cup of the Last Supper, and describing how it was taken to the *vaus d'Avaron* (vale of Avalon) in the far west by its keeper Bron, the Rich Fisher. The result is a mixture of the apocryphal history of Joseph of Arimathea with Celtic material about Bran not unlike that used by Chrétien and, most surprisingly, with Glastonbury's claims. Giraldus Cambrensis' identification of Glastonbury as Avalon in 1196, following the discovery of Arthur's body there, seems to have been known to Robert and to the author of the *Perlesvaus*, to which we shall come later. Whether it was indeed Robert who brought all these threads together, or whether he really had the source he acknowledges – 'a great book on the secret called the Grail' – we cannot tell. There are glaring contradictions and references to other writings about the Grail which suggest some kind of careless collation from a number of authors; but the idea alone of combining the different elements is a stroke of genius in itself.

Almost as bold is the idea of the *Merlin* (which can be reconstructed from a later prose version), as a sequel to the holy history. Merlin is born as a result of a plot by the devil to outwit the Messiah, and is the child of a virgin and an incubus, a parallel to the opening of *Joseph d'Arimathie* in which the birth of Christ is related. Merlin is saved from his devilish ancestor by his mother, and this leads into the stories of his work in Britain for Uther Pendragon and Arthur, culminating in the foundation of the Round Table and the coronation of Arthur.

Within a decade or two, perhaps following a plan outlined by

Robert de Boron, the story of Arthur and the achievement of the Grail quest were combined in a further poem, of which only a prose version, the so-called *Didot Perceval*, survives. The account of Perceval's success in the Grail quest is borrowed in part from Chrétien de Troyes and his continuators; the rest of the detail is dictated by the events in *Joseph d'Arimathie*. The final pages describing Arthur's Roman triumphs and last conflict with Mordred are borrowed from the pseudo-historical tradition, and contain no mention of Lancelot and Guinevere. The story as here presented thus lacks one of its major themes, and has in any case come down to us only in fragments or late versions; if Robert de Boron and his followers represent an important step forward in the Arthurian tradition, what survives of their work today is chiefly of interest to scholars.

The orthodox version of the story of Arthur, as far as medieval readers were concerned, was that contained in the Vulgate Cycle. This consisted of five romances, corresponding to the divisions of Robert de Boron's cycle, but with the *Lancelot* in the centre. *The History of the Holy Grail* repeats the adventures of Joseph of Arimathea and is followed by the *Merlin*, taken almost directly from Robert's version but with a lengthy sequel, which sometimes varies in content. The new material is contained in the *Lancelot*, the *Quest for the Holy Grail* and the *Mort Artu*, and almost all of it stems from Lancelot's new place as the most important secular Arthurian hero. Besides Chrétien's *Knight of the Cart*, Lancelot had also appeared as the central figure of a German poem, Ulrich von Zatzikhoven's *Lanzelet*, itself taken from a lost Anglo-Norman romance. The story of his birth and upbringing by the Lady of the Lake comes from this source; as with Arthur and Perceval, there is a magical or mysterious element in his origins. This is linked by a long series of adventures to the plot of Chrétien's poem, in which the author tries to minimise the guilt of Lancelot and Guinevere towards Arthur, just as the later writers tried to reduce the offence of Tristan and Isolt by blackening Mark's character. The author of *Lancelot* goes about his work more subtly. Arthur forgets to grind on Lancelot's sword at his knighting and this is done by Guinevere, thus establishing a bond of feudal loyalty between them, which is soon deepened by physical attraction.

And Lancelot and Guinevere become lovers on the night when Arthur sleeps with the enchantress Camille. Arthur then repudiates Guinevere in favour of the false Guinevere, a magical creation of Morgan le Fay, thus further weakening his claim to her loyalty.

Two techniques which Chrétien and Robert de Boron had begun to use experimentally are brought to fruition by the writer of the Vulgate Cycle: the interweaving of adventures and the introduction of events which foreshadow future developments, which the characters of the romance fail to recognise but which are evident to the reader. In the section leading up to the consummation of Lancelot's love for Guinevere, Lancelot's adventures are interwoven with those of Galehault, who plays an important part in bringing the pair together. The action then turns to the preparation for the Grail quest, in which Lancelot begets the new Grail hero, after marvels have made it clear that he will soon be supplanted as the best knight of the world because of his unchastity.

Turning to the *Quest* proper, this is now closely linked with the Round Table. The Grail appears at Arthur's Court at Pentecost, on the same day that Galahad arrives there and passes the test of the Siege Perilous, the seat at the Round Table which slays anyone who dares to sit on it unless he is destined to occupy it. The events of the *Quest* are greatly altered from the *Didot Perceval* and Chrétien, and concentrate as much on the failure of the once invincible heroes of Arthur's Court, Lancelot and Gawain, as on the success of Galahad, Perceval and Bors. The Grail is entirely spiritual in meaning, and there is a strong ascetic feeling behind the attitude towards it which suggests that a monk of the Cistercian order may have shaped this part of the Cycle. A new ideal has supplanted the secular chivalry in which the Lady of the Lake lovingly instructed Lancelot, and the knights are now judged by how nearly they approach sainthood. The adventures, too, draw heavily on Biblical tradition and symbolism; the ship which takes the knights to the accomplishment of the Quest is an allegory of the Church, and there are echoes of the Messiah in the figure of Galahad. Each step in the progress of the knights is expounded by hermits, with whom they hold long conversations, and the doctrines they teach correspond closely to the ideals of the Cistercians. This radical rethinking of the idea of the Grail from the hints and half thought out ideas of earlier writers reaches its culmination in the scene at the Castle of Corbenic. The Celtic mysteries are translated into religious ecstasy. The knights achieve, not the solution of a riddle or the breaking of a spell, but divine grace itself through the Grail as fount of the Eucharist; and the final scenes of the *Quest* achieve an irresistible power as a vision of man's aspiration towards a higher existence, that existence into which Galahad and Perceval pass, leaving Bors to ride homeward and bear the message of their success to Arthur's disheartened and depleted Court.

Just as the Grail has been given a high moral meaning, so the last part of the story, the *Mort Artu*, is changed from an illustration of the working of Fate, the fall of a great king in his hour of triumph, to the decay of a Court where spiritual values are absent. The ideals of secular chivalry, however noble, are not enough. Lancelot, who has achieved a partial vision of the Grail in token of his sincere repentance, slides back into his old sin. In episodes which echo the story of Tristan and Isolt, Lancelot rescues Guinevere from the punishment that awaits her adultery, but in so doing breaks the bonds that unite the Round Table, and allows the self-seeking Mordred to rise to power: for the first time Mordred appears as Arthur's incestuous son, and thus the king's doom is brought about by his own sin. The chain of causes seems endless and inevitable; only the spiritual way offers an escape from the toils of the flesh, and this is no longer open. Arthur, mortally wounded, is not carried to Avalon, but to burial at the Noire Chapelle; and here the remnant of his knights foregather to atone for the past in a religious life, including Lancelot, with whose death the tale ends.

We have spoken up to now of the 'author' of the Vulgate Cycle as though this huge work came from one pen. It seems likely that one man may have conceived the whole outline of the Cycle, but that it was executed by others, particularly the *Quest* and the *History of the Holy Grail*. Only a single outline could have achieved the remarkable working together of so many conflicting themes and such diverse material into a unified whole. If Lancelot's pre-eminence is the most striking new feature, Arthur is nonetheless the figure who draws the whole work together. Here for the first time the Round Table acquires a definite purpose as a secular path to virtue in a chaotic world, a means of righting wrongs and combating evil. There is a purpose behind the adventures, which they largely lacked in Chrétien's world, which derives from this sense of mission. For much of the time, Arthur has no function in the story except as the central figure of the Round Table, and only in the opening and closing sections does he become a clear-cut figure. But his role is that of a great tragic figure rather than of a paragon of chivalry, and it is this which may have led the writer to elaborate the figure of Lancelot. For each character is in some measure a representative of a particular moral function: Arthur stands for royalty and leadership; Lancelot, human achievement through chivalry; Gawain, human nature which has not come to terms with chivalry. The three Grail knights correspond to varying degrees of spiritual perfection. Galahad attains to this perfection; Perceval achieves redemption through innocent faith; while Bors reaches it through good works by which he expiates his one venial sin.

Yet had the Arthurian cycle been merely symbolic, it would never have reached such a wide audience. For the writers succeeded in making their heroes intensely human figures within their higher role. Lancelot's previously rather dutiful love for Guinevere becomes more real and passionate, and Guinevere, if there is less of the goddess about her, is a warm and human partner. Gawain's faults are not those of unrelieved wickedness, but of unrestrained passion; he cannot see the higher ideals, blinded by his immediate desires and hatreds. Even the passionless Galahad has a scene of great tenderness with his father Lancelot towards the end of the Grail quest.

It is this variety of qualities which raises the Vulgate Cycle above all other attempts at Arthurian romance on a large scale, attempts such as the *Perlesvaus* and the *Prose Tristan*. The *Perlesvaus* is an interesting and imaginative work, which may have suggested some of the themes of the Vulgate Cycle, which it probably antedates by a decade or two. It draws Arthur's own mission even further into the spiritual arena than the *Quest for the Holy Grail* by making the Grail

83

quest depend on Arthur's adherence to the New Law, the teaching of the New Testament as opposed to the Old Law of the Jews and heathens. Arthur himself has a vision of the Grail after its achievement by Perlesvaus (Perceval). The three quests of Lancelot, Gawain and Perlesvaus draw on a wide variety of earlier Arthurian material, including some Welsh sources, particularly in the description of the strange Castle of the Four Horns at which Perlesvaus ends his life. But the ideal which inspires the story is very different from that of the *Quest*. The New Law is to be imposed by force, and it belongs to the function of knights and secular rulers rather than missionaries, echoing the belligerent view of Christian missionary work found in the thinking of the Teutonic Knights. Not surprisingly, the romance lacks the humanity of the Vulgate Cycle, but it is notable as the first attempt to equate the secular mysteries of the early material with religious mysteries, and thus to give them a spiritual substance.

If the *Perlesvaus* stands at the religious extreme of Arthurian romance, the *Prose Tristan* is in ways its secular opposite. It is a vast elaboration on the nucleus provided by the story of Tristan and Isolt; introduced by a long section on Tristan's ancestry, it includes an even longer passage of Arthurian adventures while Tristan is at Arthur's Court. Among its original features are the introduction of Palamedes as Isolt's unrequited lover, and of the cynical Dinadan, whose quick wit excuses his cowardice, a kind of Court jester to the ideal of chivalry. The ending, too, is altered: Mark slays Tristan with a poisoned spear as he sits harping to Isolt, and Isolt dies in Tristan's last embrace. There is no compelling and controlling theme and the technique of interweaving adventures, successfully used in the Vulgate Cycle, here meanders aimlessly. Malory, when he came to use parts of the romance in his work, seems to have abandoned the third book in disgust, after picking out from the first two a handful of incidents hundreds of pages apart and restoring them to coherence.

When the central framework of Arthurian romance was firmly established, later writers used it once more as Chrétien had done, as the starting point for independent stories to which it was no more than a backdrop. But few if any of these offerings have the power and consistency of his work, tending rather to immense repetitive length, with endless variations on more or less meaningless events and tournaments in the manner of the *Prose Tristan*. But medieval audiences read such compilations with delight; works with a single coherent theme and structure were not necessarily so admired as these vast formless tracts of knightly exploits. A few of the late romances might appeal to a modern audience: though Renart de Beaujeu's *Le Bel Inconnu*, a tale similar to Malory's *Tale of Gareth*, which has a simple dignity, is much less typical than the 30,000 verses of *Claris and Laris* or Jean Froissart's *Meliador*. The better verse romances, by modern tastes, are those modelled on Chrétien, which freely borrow from him and from each other, and rarely have much originality. One of the stranger of the prose romances, however, deserves a brief mention, as it is the only work to present Arthur as a knight-errant hero. *Le Chevalier du Papegau* (*The Knight of the Parrot*) offers the entertaining spectacle of the noble king led on his adventures by a talking parrot in a gilded cage. The usual gamut of fantastic creatures and happenings are encountered and duly overcome, including such marvels as a Fish-Knight, whose armour, shield and horse are all part of his body and bleed when cut.

Even though few new Arthurian romances were written after 1400, they enjoyed a considerable vogue well into the sixteenth century, until the classical and Italian tradition came to dominate French literature. At the end of the fifteenth century, the French royal library contained more than thirty romances in a total collection of twelve hundred manuscripts. Huge illuminated versions were copied for Jacques d'Armagnac in the mid-fifteenth century and new compilations made for the Burgundian Court. With the advent of printing, almost all the important romances appeared as books, and many were reprinted frequently until the mid-sixteenth century. But because these late romances, and even the Vulgate Cycle itself, were formidable in extent, once the fashion for them died away, revival was vastly more difficult in France than elsewhere, particularly since it was in France that the classical tradition took the deepest hold on literature. Rabelais, sounding the death-knell of so much medieval tradition, was not so wide of the mark when he described the fate of the knights in Hell:

Lancelot of the lake was a flayer of dead horses. All the Knights of the round Table were poore day-labourers, employed to rowe over the rivers of Cocytus, Phlegeton, Styx, Acheron and Lethe, when my Lords, the devils had a minde to recreate themselves upon the water, as in the like occasion are hired the boatmen at Lions, the gondeleers of Venice, and oares at London; but with this difference, that these poor Knights have only for their fare a bob or flirt on the nose, and in the evening a morsel of course mouldie bread.

6

Tristan and Parzival: the German Romances

How original the French poets were in their treatments of the Arthurian material, we shall probably never know; the exact nature of the stories from which they worked is too obscure. With the German poets, on the other hand, there is little difficulty; with one exception, there is small room for doubt about the source from which they drew. Just as the *minnesänger* had derived their ideas about courtly love from the troubadours, so the German poets looked westwards for their inspiration in their romances, and accepted France as the arbiter of fashion.

Eilhart von Oberge's *Tristan* of about 1170, which has already been briefly discussed, is the earliest of the German poems. In common with later writers he seems to have simplified the original lost *Tristan* in the process of translation, frequently curtailing psychological explanations and occasionally distorting the plot as a result. He blames the plight of the lovers on the love-potion, and treats the tale as an adventure rather than a study of emotions. The poem's chief interest lies in its preservation of the bare outline of the first *Tristan*.

Hartmann von Aue, too, simplifies the elaborate monologues of his source, Chrétien de Troyes, but enriches his material in other directions. He came from the borders of southern Germany and Switzerland, and probably wrote his *Erek* in the last decade of the twelfth century, some thirty years after Chrétien. It is the splendours of knighthood's estate which he prefers to Chrétien's poetic economy of detail, and he expands the text with long descriptions of the marvels of his hero's equipment of the luxuries of a great feast. The result is, curiously, simpler: Chrétien's subtle characterisation disappears under the elaborate trappings, and is replaced by an insistence on the high nature of knighthood and the glamour of its world. Hartmann followed this some years later with *Iwein*, a treatment in similar vein of *Yvain*; the details are perhaps less lavish, but more acutely observed, as though the composition of two romances of his own had in the meanwhile, sharpened his vision. What we can admire is his technical skill, which was of a very high order. Hartmann's verse dazzled his would-be imitators; relying on poetic fireworks, they failed to see that his poems had a strong central plot, and the results became increasingly diffuse.

If the German writers took over their matter relatively unchanged, the greatest of them infused into the romances a far higher and more coherent ideal of knightly behaviour than Chrétien had ever attained. Wolfram von Eschenbach and Gottfried von Strassburg, in very different ways, share a spiritual approach to their subject which only the French *Quest for the Holy Grail* can begin to rival. Wolfram combines the highest philosophical themes and adventures in the manner of Chrétien with consummate skill in his *Parzival*, written in the first decade of the thirteenth century. Within the framework of romance, he portrays a world in which chivalry becomes an ideal fulfilling all man's highest aspirations, crowned by its own religious order, the knights of the Grail, and which is nonetheless real and actual.

Wolfram was a Bavarian knight, from the village now known as Wolframseschenbach. His family were *ministeriales*, knights in imperial service who remained officially serfs. Of his life we know only what he himself tells us: that he was poor – 'at home the mice rarely have enough to eat' – that he had various misfortunes in love (though he implies that he was hardly married in the end), that he was widely travelled in Germany. He came at some point in his journeyings to the Court of Hermann of Thuringia, where other great poets such as Walter von der Vogelweide had been honoured guests. His view of courtly life is not entirely approving; he has some sharp words for the disorderliness of Hermann's halls, where every insolent fellow who pretended to sing or make verses gained easy entrance. Addressing Hermann Linself, he says 'you would need someone like Keye [who appears in the romances as an uncompromising and forthright seneschal] to deal with an unruly mob like that'. And in another passage he attacks the morals that all too often lay behind the outward show of courtly love, saying that he would not care to take his wife to King Arthur's Court, where everyone's thoughts were always occupied with love. 'Someone would soon be telling her that he was transfixed by love for her, and blind with the joy it caused him; if she could cure his pain, he would always serve her. I should take her away from there before anyone had a chance to do this.' Wolfram's wry humour marks him as a man with a down-to-earth view of life, at first blush an unlikely guide through the exotic forests and spellbound adventures of his chosen subject.

The theme which Wolfram makes central to the story, Parzival's courtly and spiritual progress, is only vaguely explored in Chrétien. The old folk-tale of the prince brought up in ignorance, the 'pure fool' of noble birth, was merely another inherited *motif* from the Celtic past which served as a starting point for the romance. Wolfram turns this into a deeply-felt heroic example, yet does not preach or point a conscious moral. Indeed, his portrait of Parzival's innocence is delightful and natural. The boy, kept from the ways of knighthood that have caused his father's death, is brought up by his mother in the depths of the forest with no knowledge of the glittering world that is his birthright, with no knowledge of even the simplest ideas about life: he has learnt who God is, and that 'his love helps all who live on earth'. When he meets a knight who has fled deep into the forest to escape his pursuers, he can only imagine that this superior being is God: and though he is duly disillusioned, his natural instinct for knighthood has been aroused.

Wolfram makes great play with the idea that nobility is an inherited trait. Parzival's nature predisposes him to knighthood. From his father's family he inherits love as his destiny: from his mother's, the service of the Grail. This idea of a place in life, at once foreordained and inherited, is at the root of Wolfram's concept of society, which he sees as a series of orders crowned by knighthood.

Man should not question his appointed lot, even if it be a less honourable one than knighthood.

So Parzival sets out: dressed in fool's clothing and with the briefest of advice from his mother. She hopes that his attire will draw mockery upon him and send him back to her; and he has misunderstood her advice. This provides the matter of his first adventures, and the wrongs he unwittingly inflicts will have to be atoned for later, including the killing of Ither, a knight who has done him little harm, but whose splendid armour he covets. It is not until he reaches the castle of Gurnemanz that he finds a mentor who is prepared to educate him in matters of chivalry. His fool's attire, which he still wears beneath the real armour, is taken from him, and with it his foolish ways. Gurnemanz instructs him in courtesy and, more important, in the ethics behind courtesy. 'Never lose your sense of shame' is his first precept, and the second to show compassion to those who suffer. Parzival remembers, but does not understand: he has learnt the outward forms but not the inner meaning.

His second series of exploits starts auspiciously. He wins the heart of Condwiramurs, and marries her. The contrast with Chrétien is sharp. Perceval and Blancheflor are deeply in love but their ties are only casual. Here Parzival and Condwiramurs are bound by the ideal love to which the concept of *Minne* or love-devotion aspires, the conjugal love of marriage and passionate physical love. When Condwiramurs comes to Parzival's room at dead of night to pour out her troubles to him, they do not even kiss; it is an astonishing scene, when such nocturnal adventures have only one ending in every other romance. And when they marry, their love is so ethereal, 'they so shared togetherness', that Parzival does not think of making love to her for three nights after the wedding. The strength and joy of their earthly love shines clearly through the beautiful scene when Parzival, now at the end of his adventures, comes to meet his wife at the edge of the lands of Munsalvaesche, the Grail castle, in the grey light of dawn, and finds her asleep with their twin sons. The seneschal wakes the queen. Clad in only her shift, and a sheet hastily flung round her, with one impetuous movement she is in Parzival's arms. Parzival embraces her; the children wake, and he stoops to kiss them too. The old seneschal and the attendant ladies discreetly retire with the children, and leave the pair alone to prolong the night until the sun stands high in the heavens.

In this ideal marriage Parzival fulfils one half of his nature, the steadfastness in love inherited from his father. Most heroes of romance win their ladies only at the end of the tale. Even apparent exceptions such as Erec and Yvain, do not finally secure their beloved's affection until their adventures are over, and their deeds are always carried out with the idea of gaining favour in their lady's eyes. To Parzival, Condwiramurs is both the lady of his love-service and his sustaining hope in his adventures. At one moment, like Chrétien's hero, we find him sunk in ecstasy over three drops of blood in the snow, which remind him of the complexion of his beloved. If we remember that she is also his wife, the difference between Chrétien and Wolfram is evident. The idea for this relationship may well be evolved from Chrétien's married heroes, yet it is transformed by Wolfram's complete acceptance of the situation. Chrétien cannot quite believe that knighthood and marriage are compatible; for Wolfram they are the most natural companions in the world. Even Gawan, whose adventures occupy about half the romance, and whose deeds and character are much closer to his French counterpart, ends by marrying the proud Orgeluse. Orgeluse is in the French romance an irrational, scornful figure; and it would seem difficult for even Wolfram to make her a convincing character. Yet she becomes entirely human in his hands; her pride and scorn are partly the result of the loss of her lover, partly a test by which she will find the hero who can revenge her on her lover's killer.

Parzival's other inheritance takes us into the moral and religious spheres which are notably absent from Chrétien's unfinished poem. After a time, Parzival asks Condwiramurs to let him go in search of his mother; 'loving him truly, she could not disagree', and he sets out on a quest which, though he does not know it, is to lead not to his mother, but to his fulfilment of his part as guardian of the Grail. It is a task for which he is not yet ready: for though he comes to Munsalvaesche, the Grail castle, he heeds only Gurnemanz's warning that curiosity is rude, and does not ask the crucial question on seeing

the Grail borne in procession, and the agony of the Grail-king, Anfortas. (It is noteworthy that Wolfram has his own ideas about the
Grail, which he presents as a stone of strange powers which fell from
heaven during the struggle between Lucifer and the angels, and
which has the power to attract the highest and best in men.) The
offence of the Grail-king has been to pursue earthly love without
permission, thus breaking the laws of the Grail community, and he
now lies wounded between the thighs in punishment, until such time
as an unknown knight shall come and ask him: 'Lord, what ails
thee?' Parzival may observe the outward forms of courtesy and sup-
presses his curiosity; but forgets its inward essence, humility and
compassion. He leaves the desolate castle – which had shone with
all the show of a splendid feast on the previous night – in a dark and
lonely dawn, with only the curses of the gatekeeper to speed him on
his way. As if to show that ordinary men cannot judge between
inward and outward courtesy, Parzival rides on to his greatest
triumph yet at Arthur's Court, only to have it shattered by the arrival of Cundry, the hideous messenger from the Grail castle, who
roundly curses him for his 'falseness', both to his nature and to his
destiny.

However, Parzival can only ask the question when he is spiritually
ready to do so: and his reactions to Cundry's message show that he is
far from such a state of mind or spirit. In the grip of black despair, he
curses God for not rewarding his faithful service, and departs in
search of the Grail again. He is now farther than ever from it, seeking
it despite God; the lesson he has to learn is not only compassion and
humility, but penitence and the real nature of man's relationship to
God. He sees the latter only in feudal terms as a contract by which
man's service earns God's favour. It is not until he comes, after long
wanderings, to his uncle, Anfortas' hermit brother Trevrizent, that
the way begins to clear. In Chrétien's version, Perceval is quickly
brought to penitence, and goes on his way with no more than a brief
lesson and prescribed penance.

Wolfram makes this scene the crux of his hero's development. The
pilgrims who reproach him for bearing arms on Good Friday bring
him out of the heedless, timeless mood in which he declares that 'he

once served a lord called God, until He chose to scorn and disgrace me.' Though he gives his horse its head so that God may lead him to Trevrizent, he still defies and challenges: 'if this is his day for giving help, let Him help, if He is so inclined', and he only admits to his state of mind gradually, under Trevrizent's patient questioning. As his story unfolds, so does the seriousness of his offences appear: the killing of Ither, which he had dismissed as something done while 'I was still a fool', proves to be the murder of a kinsman; and his equally thoughtless desertion of his mother has caused her death from sorrow. Finally, his failure to ask the redeeming question when he was the chosen knight to do this has condemned his uncle – for such Anfortas proves to be – to continued years of pain. Parzival now sees that though he has indeed been a skilful and valiant knight, his own sins are so great that he has no claim on God; the way lies not through deeds alone, but also through belief. 'God himself is loyalty', and cannot be disloyal, which had been the burden of Parzival's complaint against him. The spiritual world cannot be conquered by earthly virtues and services. He departs, chastened; the seeds of penitence and redemption are sown.

When 'the story comes to its rightful theme' again, Parzival and Gawan fight a duel as strangers, in which Parzival is victor, though – as usual in the romances – he recognises Gawan before they have done each other serious injury. A similar combat ensues with Parzival's half-brother Feirefiz, in which the combatants are equally matched; again, they recognise each other in time. In the meanwhile, he has also fought a mutual enemy of his and Gawan's, Gramoflanz. Each of these battles at this stage of Parzival's spiritual progress, must represent more than another episode in the romance, or they would reduce Parzival to the level of a mere knight-errant like Gawan again. But in the wider symbolism of the poem, Gawan represents earthly chivalry, and Gramoflanz pride; both earthly chivalry and pride must be overcome. And Feirefiz, Parzival's pagan half-brother from his father's marriage to the heathen Belakane, is the archetype of natural goodness; despite his strange black and white striped skin, he is as courteous as any of the knights of the Round Table, and as virtuous as any Christian. It is Feirefiz who is the one knight chosen by Parzival to go with him on his journey to claim the kingship of the Grail.

For Parzival's trials are now at an end; and on the day of Feirefiz's admission to the Round Table, a day of 'sweet pure clarity', the messenger from the Grail castle returns, to announce that he has been named as King of the Grail, letters which have appeared on the magical stone itself. He rides to Munsalvaesche; the compassionate question is asked, Anfortas healed. The story moves swiftly to its end, telling how Condwiramurs rejoins Parzival, how Feirefiz is converted and married to the bearer of the Grail, Repanse de Schoye, and how Loherangrin succeeds his father. The two ways are reconciled: earthly and spiritual chivalry move in harmony.

Parzival is at once the greatest and most human figure in the romances; in him the highest ideal of chivalry is shot through with a warmth and natural ease which owes little to convention. By contrast, Gawan, the secondary hero of the story, is a formal figure, moving within a limited world, but perfect within his own established limits. The idea of *orden*, levels of achievement according to each man's power, enables Wolfram to transcend the old ideals of knighthood, and to set a higher goal without contradicting these cherished images. For this is his real insight: that the chivalry underlying the stories is not merely a matter of rules of good behaviour, of a code of courtly love, or even of religious service. Its strength lies in its appeal to man's better nature while remaining in close contact with the realities of life. The marvellous is only an outward trapping, corresponding to the splendours of Court festivals; what matters is the effect of these great ideals on the mind and soul. Chrétien had started to explore the effect of idealism in love on men's minds; in *Parzival*, Wolfram extends and completes the search, until his framework of an imaginary world contains the history of the way of Everyman to Salvation.

Wolfram's disrespect for courtly conventions, his inventiveness, sly humour, and obscure and uneven style, won him harsh words from his great contemporary, Gottfried von Strassburg. In the middle of his *Tristan*, Gottfried breaks off to discuss his fellow poets, and the only one whom he cannot praise is 'the friend of the hare', as he calls

94

Wolfram: the breadth of Wolfram's ideas, as well as his weakness for strange pieces of second-hand alchemists' lore, earned him that title. Gottfried is single-minded by comparison, and his purpose is quite different; so different as to be almost diametrically opposite.

The versions of the story of Tristan and Isolde we have looked at so far have been largely unpolished, relying on the elemental power of the tale for their effect; Thomas has been the only poet to begin to adapt it to other ends. From this rough stone, Gottfried carves and polishes one of the masterpieces of erotic literature. Wolfram raises chivalry's idealism to its highest peak: Gottfried takes courtly love and infuses it with pure passion. The result is a work within the broad tradition of the romances, but which breaks some of the conventional rules by the very nature of the subject matter.

Like *Parzival, Tristan* begins with an account of the hero's father and his exploits. But as soon as Tristan himself appears, there is a great gulf fixed between the two tales. Parzival is potentially perfect, and seeks to fulfil that perfection; Tristan can do no wrong from the moment he is born. Image beyond all words of the perfect courtier and knight, every skill is at his command, no virtue is too taxing. Strong, handsome, gay, he turns his hand to chess, harping, the arts of venery or war, speaks several languages, is at ease from the moment he sets foot in a strange Court.

With such a beginning, we might well expect to find ourselves back in the world of Chrétien, amidst yet more extravagant fantasies. Instead, the fantasies are kept to a minimum; the descriptions are extraordinarily real, yet none the less beautiful for it. The courtly world needs no apology, no excusing ethos; for Gottfried it is normal and natural. Tristan's loyalty to Mark, his duty to his subjects as ruler of Parmenie are part of this world; his adventures, until he meets Isolde, are purely chivalrous and of a very simple type. The slaying of Morold is treated in an antique heroic manner, as is the theme of the poisoned sword whose wounds only the dead man's relatives can heal.

Gottfried uses this perfect, self-contained world only as a starting-point. As with Wolfram, there are higher ends in view. Wolfram looks to a perfection to be gained by striving and effort, and spiritual pilgrimage; Gottfried's higher world is very different. Tristan and Isolde are already perfect. It is this that qualifies them for the transcending experience. The mysticism of love is his theme, and he speaks only to those 'noble hearts' who can understand his message.

The crux of the story, the famous scene where Tristan and Isolde drink the love-potion, thinking it is common wine, has been given many different meanings. Gottfried uses the idea skilfully. He leaves us uncertain whether the drink merely confirms a love already begun, or is in itself the *coup de foudre*. For his own purposes he is well enough content to let it be regarded as a supernatural force; with this excuse he can tell his story of open adultery, treachery and broken oaths as a special case, and invoke magic as the cause of each transgression. On the other hand, the 'noble hearts' who understood his true meaning could see the potion merely as surrogate of love's power, a symbol of its workings.

Tristan and Isolde's love puts their relationship above the everyday ways of the world. They are no longer subject to the ordinary laws of men, and can only be judged in terms of their fidelity to each other and to love's ideals. The conflict and tension that arises between the two worlds, their unresolved discontent, shows that this is not an intensified version of courtly love, but a more disturbing force. Passion is the word we have now come to use for this force, and it is a commonplace of our view of love. But to Gottfried's contemporaries, despite Chrétien's tentative descriptions of the symptoms, this was novelty indeed.

Tristan and Isolde are equal in love. There is no question of knight serving lady; instead, they are both servants of *Frau Minne*, Lady Love. Caution becomes impossible, compromise unthinkable once her mystic joys have been tasted. Love becomes the fountain of all goodness, and even provides them with physical sustenance. The climax of the poem is the episode in which the lovers, banished by Mark, take refuge in the *'fossiure à la gent amant'*, the Cave of Lovers. In this symbolically perfect retreat, whose every feature corresponds to one of Love's qualities: 'Their high feast was Love, who gilded all their joys; she brought them King Arthur's Round Table as homage and all its company a thousand times a day! What better food could they have for body or soul? Man was there with Woman, Woman there with Man. What else should they be needing? They had what they were meant to have, they had reached the goal of their desire.'

But if love is a higher ideal than those of the courtly world in which the lovers move, it affords them no protection. Its joys are balanced by its sorrows; and its sorrows stem from the lovers' concern for their reputation. When Mark discovers them lying with a naked sword between them and is persuaded of their innocence, they return to Court 'for the sake of God and their place in society'. Mark represents the opposite side of love: lust and appetite aroused by Isolde's beauty, As such he cannot find peace either; a pitiful figure, he wavers between the unpalatable truth and the comfort of illusion. Despite its outward gaiety, the Court of Cornwall which he rules is similarly tainted; suspicion is everywhere, misunderstanding and distrust abound. Only Brangane and Kurvenal remain loyal; and even their steadfastness is tested. Isolde, fearing lest Brangane should reveal their secrets, tries to have her killed, but repents as soon as she fears the deed is really done. For loyalty only exists between the lovers themselves; all external claims are brushed aside and there is left.

A man, a woman; a woman, a man:
Tristan, Isolde; Isolde, Tristan.

Their true world is an enclosed, charmed garden, the garden of the Cave of Lovers; in the every day world, no matter how splendid and gay, they move guiltily, forced to deny their desires, and the air grows thick with sorrow and evil.

Gottfried did not complete his poem; whether by design or accident, we cannot tell for certain. It ends with Tristan's thoughts as he is torn between the idea of marrying Isolde of the White Hands, whose love he has won during his self-imposed exile from Cornwall, or remaining single for Isolde of Ireland's sake; and it seems likely that Gottfried was similarly torn between faithfully following the story as given in his original, and the loyalty in love which had become both his main theme and the excuse for his hero and heroine's misdeeds. That this ideal meant a great deal to him is plain enough, and there are veiled references to personal experiences of such a love throughout the poem. Yet, even as a guiding light for those 'noble hearts' to whom he addresses himself, it is an uncertain star. Gottfried makes sensual love sublime by his artistry; it is the one way in which the great tale he tells can come to life, but the philosophy of it is incomplete and less subtle than that of the troubadours and *minnesangers*. Indeed, it is scarcely a philosophy at all, though Gottfried would like us to think it was; it is a mysticism without a goal, the exaltation of emotion to the level of the divine through the element of suffering that emotion arouses. What he does tell us a great deal about is the psychology of love, how lovers behave and how their minds work; and his audience of 'noble hearts' are lovers who seek to find distraction for their own sorrows and perhaps a reflection of their own dilemmas.

In this lies the sharp distinction between Gottfried and Wolfram. Gottfried is a superb poet, a master of style whose cadences ring true, describing the deepest secrets of the emotions in a story well suited to his ends; Wolfram is less technically accomplished, but has a far broader view of life, which he expresses amidst the unlikely paraphernalia of knightly romance. Both, however, have risen too far beyond the conventions of the world about which they were writing for their successors to do more than admire their lofty concepts and produce imitations of the outward forms from which the inner spirit is lacking. Wolfram and Gottfried represent a *ne plus ultra*. All that is left for later writers in this genre is to compile immense fantasies, drawing on the inherited stock-in-trade of endless combats, strange adventures, mysterious beautiful damsels, prolonged quests that never seem to reach an end.

The most interesting of the lesser German romances, however, is an exception in that it precedes Wolfram and Gottfried. Ulrich von Zatzikhoven's *Lanzelet* has already been mentioned as preserving stories from which the French Vulgate Cycle was drawn. Translated from an Anglo-Norman original about 1190 in south Germany, its account of the birth and upbringing of Lancelot repeats the pattern of mystery about the origins of heroes we have noted elsewhere. But

Lancelot's later career is here presented in very different fashion. He acts briefly as Guinevere's champion, but seems to be married before he arrives at Arthur's Court. Various adventures ensue, including the abduction of Guinevere, who is only regained by the intervention of a wizard, and the disenchantment of a damsel, who appears as a dragon, by Lancelot kissing her. The story ends with Lancelot's reunion with his wife and return to his kingdom. The various individual incidents are found elsewhere in European folklore; but neither the structure nor the style rise above the mediocre.

The later German romances, like the French, became lengthy and repetitive, with the additional handicap of being in verse. There was no equivalent to the French Vulgate Cycle; though manuscripts of a German translation of this have recently come to light, they are curiosities which do not represent a widespread tradition. What we have instead are conscious attempts to invent new Arthurian romances, rather in the spirit of *Durmart le Gallois* or *Le Chevalier du Papegau*. Wirnt von Grafenberg's *Wigalois*, written *c.* 1200–10, is based on Hartmann and Wolfram, taking a definite moral attitude in the same way as the latter, but lacking his firm control of the matter in hand; the result is naïve and rather inconsequential. *Diû Krone*, written in Austria about 1220–30, by Heinrich von dem Türlin, comes under the heading of compendium romances: it is an *omnium gatherum* of all kinds of Arthurian themes, including a Grail quest with Gawain as its unexpected hero.

The immense vogue which Arthurian literature enjoyed in thirteenth-century France spread outwards to the very edges of Europe. A series of Dutch romances of the late thirteenth and early fourteenth century were chiefly based on the Vulgate Cycle, though there is one surprising work, *Walewein*, which includes Gawain's adventures with a talking fox. Three Latin romances contain some original material, but for the most part these far-flung translations were taken more or less directly from the French, whether in the Portuguese *Demanda do Santa Graal* or in the poems translated by Brother Robert for King Haakon of Norway about 1230 from Chrétien's poems, the *Erex saga* and *Ivans saga*, and from the *Tristan*. There is even a Hebrew translation of a variant of the Vulgate Cycle dating from 1279. The English romances, discussed in the next chapter, offer a mixture of direct translation, with a few pieces which seem to draw again on the Celtic stories from which all this literary activity had sprung.

As a result, the Arthurian heroes became household names throughout Europe, their adventures read by nobles and aspiring bourgeois alike. When Dante came to describe the ill-starred love of Paolo da Rimini for his sister-in-law Francesca, he made their love-potion an Arthurian romance:

> One day we read for pastime how in thrall
> Lord Lancelot lay to love, who loved the Queen;
> We were alone – we thought no harm at all.
>
> As we read on, our eyes met now and then,
> And to our cheeks the changing colour started,
> But just one moment overcame us – when
>
> We read of the smile, desired of lips-long-thwarted,
> Such smile, by such a lover kissed away,
> He that may never more from me be parted
>
> Trembling all over, kissed my mouth. I say
> The book was Galleot[1], Galleot the complying
> Ribald who wrote; we read no more that day.

There is little trace of Italian versions of the legends, except at the relatively popular level of ballads and recited poems in the repertory of the *cantastorie*. The epics of the early Renaissance include many references, direct and indirect, to the Matter of Britain, but it was Roland and Godfrey de Bouillon who provided Ariosto and Tasso with their subject-matter in *Orlando Furioso* and *Gerusalemme Liberate*, while Arthur languished in the obscurity of Alamanni's *L'Avarchide*.

A similar late flowering of heroic themes took place in Spain, the form being the romance rather than the epic. The most famous of the Spanish romances is *Amadis de Gaula*, which, in the course of its immense length and many sequels has references to Arthur; and it was as popular as it was long-winded in the telling, for the tables were now turned and the French took their reading from the Spanish, and *Amadis* was admired throughout Europe. When Cervantes came to 'smile Spain's chivalry away', he had something to say both about the romances and about Arthur, who appears in a very unexpected guise; he is said to survive in the shape of the raven. As for the romances,

> When they want to describe a battle, first they tell us that there are a million fighting men on the enemy's side. But if the hero of the book is against them, inevitably, whether we like it or not, we have to believe that such and such a knight gained the victory by the valour of his strong arm alone. Then what are we to say of the ease with which a hereditary Queen or Empress throws herself into the arms of an unknown and wandering knight? What mind not totally barbarous and uncultured can get pleasure from reading that a great tower, full of knights, sails out over the sea like a ship before a favourable wind, and that one night it is in Lombardy and by dawn next morning in the land of Prester John of the Indies . . .? If you reply that the men who compose such books write them as fiction, and so are not obliged to look into fine points or truths, I should reply that the more it resembles the truth the better the fiction, and the more probable and possible it is, the better it pleases. . . . What is more, their style is hard, their adventures are incredible, their love-affairs lewd, their compliments absurd, their battles long-winded, their speeches stupid, their travels preposterous, and lastly, they are devoid of all art and sense, and therefore deserve to be banished from a Christian commonwealth, as a useless tribe.

And on this disenchanted note, we bid farewell to Arthur's European career, save for a brief episode or two, and turn to his fortunes in England.

7
The English Poems

The earliest of the English romances was composed at about the time when the Arthurian matter began to go out of fashion in France, half-way through the thirteenth century. The last is twenty years later than Malory's 'noble tales'; thus they cover a span of two hundred and fifty years, from 1250 to 1500. None are on the same scale as their French counterparts, and of the twenty-three that survive, only five have any degree of originality. Four derive from lost French sources, and the remaining eighteen have known originals; of the latter, five are direct English renderings of complete French works.

So most of the English Arthurian poems are translations, and we might expect them to be inferior to their originals. This proves indeed to be the case, as the English writers, perhaps handicapped by the lower level of literary development of their language, rarely manage to match the courtly and polished style of the French. And this inability to maintain a grand manner leads to a more rapid progress through the plot, instead of the leisurely pace of the French; the story is invariably shortened and simplified. The English poems are usually the work of humble writers or of amateurs, who only rarely manage to touch on the innate dramatic or psychological potential of the stories they are telling. The lack of great English masterpieces is largely due to a lack of demand: the upper classes could read the French in the original, as could any of the merchants and rich citizens; and the rise of English as the predominant language coincided with the decline of the romances. So when we do come to the one masterpiece of our native medieval Arthurian literature, *Sir*

Gawain and the Green Knight, its splendours impress us all the more deeply.

Only the directness and naïve poignancy of the English romances saves them from total oblivion, and this all too often becomes banality. The French romances, designed for reading rather than recital, could afford the heartsearchings and lengthy soliloquys of Chrétien's heroes and heroines, but such material was ill adapted to the minstrel's art. The English audiences demanded adventures and marvels; and with these they were supplied in abundance. And most of the abridgement is due to the influence of the minstrels, for none of the original or largely original English poems exceeds one thousand lines or deals with more than a single episode: this brevity and simplicity of plot was what the minstrels' audiences demanded.

With this simplification goes a marked lack of taste and sophistication. Love is little discussed, and the physical side of it is more in evidence than the psychological. The wealth of kings and princes, on the other hand, is not tacitly assumed or indicated in a discreet phrase, but is described with obvious amazement and wonder. The exaggerated and grotesque are greatly in demand, and there is a marked preference for combats with giants and monsters rather than mere human opponents.

The earliest of the English poems, from the second half of the thirteenth century, is the Kentish *Arthour and Merlin*. It is a lengthy but incomplete version of the second part of the Vulgate Cycle, which even in the original is one of the less interesting elaborations of Arthurian romance, being largely an expanded and romanticised version of Geoffrey of Monmouth. Its only merit lies in the battle scenes, which are occasionally vigorous, though the alliterative poems outshine it; and the effect is largely spoilt by excessive repetition of such descriptions over the course of half a dozen campaigns.

Romances centred on a single hero form the bulk of the Middle English repertory. *Sir Perceval of Galles* presents some interesting features. Written in the north of England in the mid-fourteenth century, it runs to over two thousand lines. As a poem, it is not particularly distinguished; but its most arresting feature is that it is the only known work in which Perceval is in no way connected with the

Grail legend. We have seen how even Chrétien de Troyes' unfinished *Conte del Graal* mentions the Grail, albeit mysteriously and briefly; and Perceval is thus associated with the Grail from the very beginning. But the great question is whether the English romance, otherwise close to Chrétien's description of Perceval's boyhood, in fact represents the original form of the story. On this there are two opposing schools of thought: one group of scholars holds that the English romance is a late form of the original story from which Chrétien's poem was taken, perhaps derived in turn from the Irish epic, *Boyish Exploits of Finn* in an Anglo-Norman version. Certain features of the latter might have suggested to Chrétien the idea of adding the Grail story. On the other hand, it has been plausibly argued that the English writer, using a copy of Chrétien's work without the continuations, adapted it to form a self-contained unit, and for that reason left out the ambiguous episode of the Grail. The end of the English version betrays some confusion, which might be the result of such an attempted adaptation. On balance, the first view seems the more probable, especially as there is an Italian poem, *Carduino*, with a similar plot, which implies the existence of a common lost original in French, which would also be a forerunner of Chrétien's *Conte del Graal*.

Sir Perceval, as it stands, is a straightforward example of a theme which recurs several times in Arthurian literature. A simpleton arrives at Court with some outrageous request, and is laughed at by some of the knights; but much to their surprise, he performs great feats and sometimes overthrows in battle those who mocked him. Another romance, *Sir Libeaus Desconus*, and Malory's *Tale of Gareth* tell a similar story, in which a newly-made knight is sent, at his own request, on an adventure with a maiden who scorns him; he performs many feats of arms for her, but only gets rebukes, until the maiden herself is rebuked for her harshness by one of the knights he has defeated for her sake. It is a story with parallels in several Celtic stories, but gains greatly in purpose when adapted to a chivalric milieu.

A small group of poems contains adventures found only in English Arthurian literature. Arthur himself is one of the heroes of *The*

Avowing of King Arthur, Sir Gawain, Sir Kay and Sir Bawdewin of Britain. It is from the north of England, contemporary with *Sir Perceval of Galles*. The story opens at Carlisle, where Arthur hears of a great boar nearby, which, with the help of the three knights mentioned, he hunts to a lair in Inglewood Forest. There they all make vows: Arthur to kill the boar single-handed before dawn, Gawain to watch all night at the haunted Tarn Wadling, Kay to ride through all the forest until daybreak, and to slay anyone who opposes him, Bawdewin never to be jealous of his wife or any other lady, never to refuse food to any man, and not to fear the threat of death. All the vows are fulfilled except Kay's; Gawain rescues him, and the poem ends with Bawdewin's explanation of the events in his life which led to his triple vow. The plot has no immediate known sources. The vows are paralleled in the 'literature of boasting', where similar oaths lead to adventures, and serve, as here, to knit together a series of knightly exploits by means of an artificial central theme.

The same characters and places are common to two other stories, the *Awntyrrs of Arthur* (*Adventures of Arthur*) and *The Wedding of Sir Gawain*. In all three, Carlisle, Inglewood Forest (near Hesketh) and Tarn Wadling, a small lake in the forest, occur. It is conceivable that in their original form all three were by the same hand, although the extant versions are very different in construction and style. The title of the *Adventures of Arthur* is misleading, for Gawain is its true hero. The ghost of the Tarn Wadling proves to be Guinevere's mother, who foretells Mordred's treachery and Arthur's end; this episode is loosely linked with a joust between Gawain and Galeron, which ends indecisively, but results in Galeron's admission to the Round Table. The sources are perhaps *The Trentals of Pope Gregory*, where a similar apparition by the Pope's mother is described, and a *chanson de geste* which supplied the outline of the combat between the two knights. Gawain's connection with Galloway is mentioned, as Galeron's quarrel with Gawain is over some lands of his there which Arthur has wrongly given to the latter. Like the other poems of this group, the writing is vigorous and realistic, but not particularly polished. *The Wedding of Sir Gawain* belongs to the Gawain poems proper, to which we shall return.

The remaining Middle English poems, apart from those about Gawain, are all translations from the French, showing little originality or literary talent on the part of their authors. Perhaps the best is *Sir Libeaus Desconus* already mentioned, a mid-fourteenth-century version of the French romance of the same name by Renart de Beaujeu, which tells a story not dissimilar from that of *Sir Perceval*. As with other late French romances, it is a compendium of marvels and adventures, some delightful, some tedious, though it avoids the excessive length of works like Froissart's *Meliador*, which ran to over twenty-eight thousand lines. Plot is all-important, and action predominates over character. Many of the motifs are common in folklore, and the final adventure, by which a lady in the guise of a serpent is disenchanted by a kiss, recurs in several other romances, where it is always attracted to a son of Gawain, as Libeaus himself proves to be. An even later translation, the fifteenth-century version of *Launfal* by Thomas Chester, harks back to Marie de France's *lai* of the same title; it follows the original closely, though the taste of the times is catered for by the addition of two passages describing a duel and a tournament.

When Sir Walter Scott turned his attention to early English poetry, his greatest praise was reserved for *Sir Tristrem*; but his enthusiasm for this rather weak version of the story of Tristan and Isolt was misplaced. It is far from being the supposed original by Thomas of Britain, but is a late thirteenth-century reworking of the story, omitting the subtleties and told in an excruciating, crude, short-lined stanza, in which the numerous rhymes dominate the sense.

Two other poems, the late fifteenth-century *Lancelot du Laik* from Scotland, and the so-called stanzaic or Harleian *Le Mort Arthur* (as opposed to the alliterative *Morte Arthure* discussed earlier) draw on the Vulgate Cycle for their material, like *Arthour and Merlin*. *Lancelot du Laik* is a fragmentary treatment of a single incident from the *Prose Lancelot*, and is the work of an over-confident poet who fails to make much of his material. *Le Mort Arthur*, a substantial version of the end of the Cycle, *La Mort Artu*, has some merit. Written in Richard II's reign, it lacks the grandeur of the alliterative poem, but has a directness and simplicity which prove effective. Malory seems to have used it in his splendid version of the same French source, addressing himself to the same audience, who were neither the French-speaking Court nor the simple folk for whom ballads were written, but the merchants and burgesses of the towns for whom French was already in the late fourteenth century something of a barrier to understanding. They demanded more than a mere summary of the plot, and much of the original characterisation and chivalric attitudes is carried over into the English version.

It is only when we reach the poems about Gawain that the imagination of the English poets is fired. Curiously, in the early French romances he is indeed of great knightly skill, but he is also lascivious, and not always courteous. To the English, he represents the flower of all courtesy and gentleness, and the figure of every virtue; the other knights, excepting only Arthur himself, are usually foils to his prowess and nobility. In maintaining this high opinion of Gawain, the English poets are continuing an older tradition than that of the French romances.

Gawain first appears in Geoffrey of Monmouth's *History of the Kings of Britain* where he is called Walgainus, and in William of Malmesbury's reference to the discovery of his grave at Walwyn's Castle in Pembrokeshire. He resembles the Gwalchmai of Welsh legend and Cuchullinn in the Irish epics. Like the latter, he possesses many of the properties of a sun-hero, such as the increase of his strength until midday and its decline thereafter. He was the real owner of Excalibur, which was originally a dazzling sun-weapon. Of all the knights of the Round Table, he has the longest connections with Arthur, save for Kay and Bedivere; and in Geoffrey of Monmouth he appears as Arthur's nephew. As a folk-tale hero, he is the central figure of primitive stories, sometimes scarcely altered from their crude originals, and cuts a less and less imposing figure as the material becomes artificial and literary.

Yet the first of the poems of which he is hero, *Sir Gawain and the Green Knight*, is the most superb literary accomplishment of medieval English Arthurian writing, one of the great masterpieces of the poetry of this period. Both in its treatment of the subject-matter and in the strength of its style and imagery, it represents the climax of

English alliterative poetry. The unique manuscript contains in addition three other poems of the same period and probably by the same writer: all are in the West Midland dialect, with a strong Scandinavian influence, which is at its most marked in *Sir Gawain and the Green Knight*. This seems to have been the first of the poems to be written, about 1370 to 1390. It has been suggested that it was commissioned by John of Gaunt, and there is strong evidence for some connection between him and the poet, if not for the actual commission. The identity of the unknown genius has long been a matter for debate. No suggestion yet put forward has gained more than a handful of supporters; attempts to marshal internal evidence, whether in the form of puns or numerology, all fail to point to a convincing case for the author's identity. All that can be said with certainty about him is that he was well acquainted with courtly life, could read Latin and French, and was probably a scholar of some merit. He might well have been, or have become, a clerk in minor orders, since his later poems are distinctly religious in tone.

The poem opens with an account of the founding of Britain, and tells us that Arthur was the greatest and most honoured of Britain's kings. The story proper then begins. Arthur is at Camelot one Christmastide, and on New Year's Day, in accordance with his custom, does not eat until some adventure has taken place; and soon a gigantic knight duly appears, entirely clad in green, and riding a green horse. He demands to see Arthur, who asks him what he wants. The knight proposes a bargain: any one of Arthur's knights who is bold enough to strike off his head with the axe he has brought, may do so — provided he will accept a return blow in a year's time. The knights, awed by the visitor's appearance, hesitate, and the Green Knight taunts them with cowardice. Arthur angrily leaps forward to take up the challenge himself, but Gawain restrains him, and asks permission to undertake the adventure himself. Arthur agrees, and Gawain beheads the Green Knight. To the astonishment of the onlookers, the latter picks up his head, which admonishes Gawain to meet him at the Green Chapel in a year's time, and gallops away with it under his arm.

Next All Hallows Day, Gawain is armed in preparation for his departure in search of the mysterious trysting place. He rides through the kingdom of Logrees to north Wales, and eventually reaches the wilderness of Wirral, by way of Anglesey, Holyhead and the coast. By now it is Christmas, and he finds himself in a vast, dreary forest. He kneels and prays, and shortly afterwards, a splendid castle appears. Here he finds shelter for the night, and learns that the Green Chapel is but a few miles distant. The lord of the castle invites him to remain until the New Year, now only three days away, and proposes a bargain: he will go hunting each day, and Gawain shall remain at the castle with his wife. At the end of each day they will exchange their spoils.

The hunts take place, with all the ceremonial that medieval huntsmen loved; and meanwhile the lady visits Gawain each morning while he is still abed and tries to seduce him in her lord's absence. He, however, turns aside her advances with courteous but artful speeches. At the end of each day, the winnings are duly exchanged: Gawain gives one kiss for several deer on the first evening, two kisses for a boar on the second. However, on the third day, the lady gives him a magical green lace girdle which protects the wearer from all harm, and three kisses as well. Gawain, by keeping this and giving the lord only the three kisses, in exchange for a fox's skin, breaks the agreement.

Early next morning, Gawain makes his way to the Green Chapel with one of the lord's servants, who warns him of the fearful strength of the Green Knight and advises him to turn back. Gawain refuses, but finding the Green Chapel deserted, is about to go, when he hears the sound of an axe being whetted, and discovers the Green Knight preparing for the encounter. Gawain bows to receive the blow, but the Green Knight accuses him of flinching when he lifts the axe. He promises to keep still, and the Green Knight lifts the axe again, but lowers it without striking. Finally he lifts it again and lets it fall in such a way that it slightly grazes Gawain's neck. He then reveals that he is the lord of the castle at which Gawain had stayed, and that his wife had tempted Gawain in accordance with his instructions. The two feints were in payment for the kisses, and the graze was for the magic lace girdle which he had kept in breach of the terms of the bargain. Gawain is ashamed at being found out, and offers to give back the girdle, but is made to keep it and wear it in memory of his disgrace. The Green Knight tells him that his name is Bercilak de Hautdesert, and that it was Morgan le Fay who had arranged the adventure in order to prove the Round Table and frighten Guinevere. Gawain returns to Arthur's Court, and, although much abashed, relates his adventures. The King decrees that all knights of the Round Table shall wear a green baldric in memory of his adventure.

In this tale there are two distinct themes which have been skilfully welded into one. The Green Knight's challenge to Gawain is an example of Celtic episode that we may call the Beheading Game. The approaches of his hostess at the castle form the other part, the Temptation. Both incidents are of great age and have a long pedigree. In the case of the Beheading Game, the earliest form of the story is to be found in the Irish epic *Bricriu's Feast*, in which it is part of the contest for the championship of Ulster, with Cuchullinn as its hero. Even here it occurs twice in variant forms, and must have come from a recited version of about the eighth century, that is two hundred years before the earliest manuscript. From Ireland it passed to France, perhaps via Wales and Brittany, and by comparing the details of those stories in which it is found, we can reconstruct the original translation. Three French romances made use of this theme: in two cases Gawain is the hero, in the third Lancelot. A second version in a rather different form appears in the *Livre de Caradoc*, and it is this adaptation which is closest to that in *Sir Gawain and the Green Knight*. The common feature of all versions is a supernatural being who is beheaded without apparent harm and who returns his half of the bargain with a harmless blow.

The Temptation story is also Celtic in origin, the nearest parallel being found in *Pwyll*, one of the stories in the Welsh *Mabinogion*. This offers three major points of resemblance: a noble huntsman who introduces the hero as guest, a temptation scene in which the huntsman's wife is repulsed by the hero, and a year's interval between a challenge incident and its sequel. The huntsman is also the same colour as his horse, grey as opposed to green in the English poem.

Two French stories also stem from a similar original: the first, in the romance *Yder*, differs considerably from the other group, for here the hero repulses the temptress physically and treats her roughly. This may go back to the primitive Irish original; the second French version is represented by the incident in *Sir Gawain and the Carl of Carlisle*, in which the host puts Gawain into his wife's bed, orders him to kiss her three times, but forbids him to go further. In reward for his obedience, he is given the host's daughter. This episode, however, belongs to the group of 'Imperious Host' stories, in which obedience is the crucial factor. The other French parallel, in the *Chevalier à l'Epée*, is confused by the introduction of other features, such as the Enchanted Bed which kills anyone who sleeps on it. A third variation, in the German *Lanzelet*, has a temptress acting of her own free will, whose advances are accepted. So the Temptation motif has no clear-cut line of descent as in the case of the Beheading Game; all we can say is that there seems to have been a French story of this type which was known to the Gawain poet.

Just when these two themes were combined has long been disputed. One school of thought favours a lost French original containing both; against this, a poet of the stature of the author of *Sir Gawain and the Green Knight* would be perfectly capable of making such a fusion. Let us for the moment accept the latter view, while remembering that the poem's merit in no way depends on it. Whoever did make the two stories one was a brilliant sculptor of poetic form; for the outcome of one part is made to depend on the other with great subtlety. The crux is the exchange of spoils during the three days' hunting, which provides a motive for the slight blow given to Gawain by the Green Knight. Gawain conceals the girdle out of fear of his encounter on the following day, which would have passed off without incident otherwise. Thus, while the Temptation arises naturally enough out of the Challenge, this addition makes the issue of the Challenge depend on the outcome of the Temptation. But such a plot is as nothing unless matched by verse and language. And here at last is an English poet writing an Arthurian romance who is capable of the task. The alliterative verse is in his hands a mirror of mood and imagination. The least description is turned into a jewel

111

of language, whether it be the details of Gawain's arming before his departure or the loving portrayal of the Green Knight's magical axe:

> A spetos sparthe to expoun   in spelle whoso might
> The hede of an elnyarde   the large lenkthe hade,
> The grain al of grene stele   and of golde hewen,
> The bit burnist bright   with a brode edge
> As wel shapen to schere   as sharp rasores.
> The stele of a stif staf   the sturne hit bi gripte
> That was wounden with iron   to the wandes ende,
> And al bigraven with grene   in gravios werkes.[1]

But the greatest passages are those in which the poet depicts Nature and her ways, a theme which underlies the poem in several aspects. Two stanzas at the opening of the second part describe the changing seasons between Christmas and Michaelmas, and surpass all conventional poetry of this kind. They are followed by the harsh weather which Gawain encounters on his journey northwards, where in the sound of the words and in the rugged rhythms the very spirit of winter echoes and re-echoes. The northern countryside in which the poet lived rises up before us in its most severe and impressive beauty. Across this background sweep past the three days' hunting, in which the essence of the chase is exactly caught: days of exhilaration, danger, triumph and noble ritual, at the end of each a homecoming to a warm welcome and a blazing fire when the last horn has been blown. On the day of the tryst at the Green Chapel, the countryside grows grim once more; the hills are mist-mantled, there is hoar-frost in the oakwoods, snow in the valleys. But perhaps the finest picture of all is that of Gawain lying awake on New Year's Day, waiting for dawn and listening to the gale outside:

> Now neghes the New Yere   and the night passes,
> The day drives to the derk   as Drighten biddes;
> Bot wilde wederes of the worlde   wakned theroute,
> Cloudes kesten kenly the colde to the erthe,
> With nighe innoghe of the northe, the naked to tene;

The snawe snitered ful snart, that snayped the wilde;
The werbelande winde   wapped fro the highe,
And drof eche dale ful   of driftes ful grete.
The leude listened ful wel   that ley in his bedde,
Thagh he lowkes his liddes, ful littel he slepes;
Bi ech kok that crue   he knew wel the steven.[2]

The people of this harsh, real world are equally alive; their feasts and merry-making, gaiety and good cheer are far from the delicate but artificial world of the French romances, and their conversations are as unforced and natural as those of the heroes and heroines of Chrétien de Troyes are studied and literary.

But just as Nature dominates the real world, so natural magic dominates the spiritual plane of the poem. The Green Knight is a superhuman being with strange powers, who moves in an aura of mystery, the shadow of his ancient role as the incarnation of spring who must be slain in winter in order to renew life for the next year. In the Temptation, he becomes a gay, friendly lord, owner of a fair castle; but this is only a disguise, even if the poet, uneasy at the pagan implications of his subject-matter, blames the whole mystery on Morgan le Fay. The strange legendary world of Norse and Saxon literature is never far from the poet's mind; Gawain encounters dragons, trolls and giants on his journey northward. The contrast between the Green Knight's two shapes is cunningly exploited, to heighten the climax of the poem.

The poet handles what was once no more than a romance with such high intent that it becomes in his treatment a moral and didactic example. Gawain, the model of knighthood, only escapes the fatal return blow because he holds out against the lady's adulterous temptations. This is a far cry from the French writers' easy acceptance, indeed exaltation, of the immorality of courtly love. They would probably have admired such a sin, even though it contravened the strictest conception of this code. Yet they would have agreed with his punishment, for by breaking his word in concealing the girdle, he has dishonoured the order of knighthood. The English poet takes even these worldly ideals onto a higher plain: Gawain's device, the pentangle, borne on his shield, is a religious rather than

113

armorial symbol, and he is frequently called 'Mary's knight'. There is an idealism throughout that raises the poem far above the level of the other English romances, and reminds one of Wolfram von Eschenbach. Gawain is an idealised hero who makes one error that cannot be redeemed, although not fatal; Parzival, on the other hand, although he almost fails in the Grail quest when he does not ask the question at his first visit to the Grail castle, gains a second opportunity by long years of atonement. The common subject of Wolfram and the Gawain poet is the search for perfection; for Wolfram it is typified by the achievement of the mysterious Grail, and in the other by the more realistic preservation of knightly honour in face of temptation. And the Gawain poet is more pessimistic than Wolfram, who sees perfection as eventually attainable; here the hero's reputation is contrasted with reality. Some writers have seen *Sir Gawain and the Green Knight* as a poem with a didactic moral; but it is rather a moral reflection on human weakness.

In this poem, the Arthurian legend leaves its realms of isolated fantasy to become natural and human; the result has the same power and pathos as the closing pages of Malory. Here language, style and a subtle framework combine into a magnificent achievement, and beside it all but a handful of Arthurian poems pale into literary insignificance. Of this handful, only Wolfram can offer the same high idealism and sustained exaltation of chivalry.

The condensed and corrupt ballad form of this masterpiece is completely unworthy of its great original. *The Green Knight* shows how the ballad makers of the late fifteenth century sought a new audience by simplifying vocabulary and plot until all save pure adventure had been stripped away. In place of the complexities of the earlier poem, the motive is provided by the improbable love of the lady of the castle for Gawain, whom she has never seen, thus diminishing the impact of the challenge episode. Indeed, the only interest this crude production can hold for us is to emphasise the heights and depths of which English romances on Arthur were capable. Here are the two descriptions of Gawain's journey to the Green Chapel; firstly, that of *The Greene Knight* and then that of *Sir Gawain and the Green Knight*:

114

When he rode over the mold,
His geere glistered as gold,
  By the way as he rode;
Many furleys there saw he,
Fowles by the water did flee,
  By brimes and bankes soe broad.

Many furleys there saw he,
Of wolves and wild beasts sikerlye,
  On hunting he tooke most heede;
Forth he rode, the sooth to tell,
For to seeke the Greene Chappell,
  He wist not where indeed.[3]

Mony clif he overclambe   in contrayes straunge,
Fer floten fro his frendes   fremedly he rides.
At eche warthe other water   ther the wighe passed
He fonde a foo him before,   bot ferly hit were,
And that so foule and so felle   that feght him behode.
So mony mervayl bi mount   ther the mon findes,
Hit were to tore for to telle   of the tenthe dole.
Sumwhile with wormes he werres,   and with wolves als,
Sumwhile with wodwos,   that woned in the knarres,
Bothe with bulles and beres   and bores otherwhile
And etaines that him anelede   of the heghe felle;
Nade he ben dughty and drighe,   and Drighten had served
Douteless he hade ben ded   and dreped ful ofte.
For werre wrathed him not so much,   that winter was wors,
When the colde cler water   Fro the cloudes shadde,
And fres er hit falle might   to the fale erthe;
Ner slain with the slete   he sleped in his yrnes
Mo nightes then innoghe   in naked rokkes,
Ther as claterande fro the crest   the colde borne rennes,
And henged heghe over his hede   in hard iise-ikkles
Thus in peril and paine   and plites ful harde
Bi contray cayres this knight,   til Kristmasse even,
                all one;
        The knight wel that tide
        To Mary made his mone,
        That ho him red to ride
        And wisse him to sum wone.[4]

The beheading incident which is the main episode of *Sir Gawain and the Green Knight* recurs in various forms in several other poems with Gawain as hero. The fragmentary *Turk and Gawain* seems to have come fairly directly from a Celtic folk-tale, Irish or perhaps Manx in origin. An enchanted knight in the shape of a dwarf or 'turk' issues a challenge to Gawain in order to get the latter to break the spell on him by beheading him. The background and any other description are reduced to a bare minimum, in order to concentrate on the plot, and only one other figure, Sir Kay, 'that crabbed knight', appears as a foil to Gawain. The plot and a few scant details suggest that it may well be an Arthurian adaptation of a folk tale from Ireland made by some northern poet.

Sir Gawain and the Carl of Carlisle embodies a similar test and disenchantment story, and is a good example of the material of this group of 'primitive' romances. Arthur and his knights go hunting, and Bishop Baldwin, Kay and Gawain pursue a deer by themselves, and lose their way. They come to the castle of the Carl of Carlisle, of which, so Baldwin tells them, it is said that no man ever stayed there and escaped with his life. Nonetheless, they enter, and meet the Carl, a hideous giant who keeps a bear, a boar, a bull and a lion in his hall. Gawain is always courteous and obedient to his host, while the others break all the rules of good conduct. He is asked by the Carl to throw a spear at him, which he duly does; the Carl dodges the missile, and then, leading Gawain to his wife's chamber, puts him in her bed and bids him kiss three times, but not more. He then leads him to his daughter, with whom he spends the night. The next morning, the Carl orders Gawain to cut off his head, which the latter reluctantly does; whereupon the Carl changes into an ordinary man, and explains how he had been enchanted until such time as a knight should arrive who would obey his commands. Any knight who refused to obey him had been killed. Gawain weds the Carl's daughter, and the Carl is made a knight of the Round Table.

This short romance appears to be based on an Irish or Celtic story, translated directly from the original. The nearest parallel is the Irish *Curoi's Castle*, in which the giant also has four beasts, the hero's companions fail the test, and the hero is made to hurl a spear at the giant. The framework of the romances is the Imperious Host motif, found in every European folklore. In tales of this kind, anyone arriving at the host's castle who does not implicitly obey his word, even if good manners would seem to require disobedience, is automatically killed. This trial would be an obvious qualifying test for the disenchantment by decapitation; and at bottom *The Turk and Gawain* and *Sir Gawain and the Carl of Carlisle* are different versions of the same story.

The last poem of this group is *The Wedding of Sir Gawain and Dame Ragnell*, whose plot, the story of the loathly bride who must win a handsome husband in order to be released from a spell, is one of the commonest of folktales and is best known in the form of Chaucer's *Wife of Bath's Tale*. The ballad version is of course much less interesting than Chaucer's account of it, where the episode is sparked off by an incident from *The Gest of Sir Gawain*, the rape of Brandelis' sister. As punishment, Gawain must answer the question 'What do women most desire?'; and this leads into the plot of *The Wedding of Sir Gawain*, in which Gawain is suitably chastised by having to marry the hag who solves his problem. But Chaucer lets him off lightly; he is given the choice of having a bride who is faithful and ugly, or one who is beautiful but wayward. It is only by remembering the answer to the question – women most desire mastery over men – and allowing his bride to choose, that she becomes both beautiful and faithful.

All three ballads may represent a local cycle of poems about Gawain, perhaps from the same area as *Sir Gawain and the Green Knight*. There is evidence for survival of a sizeable Celtic population in Cumberland and Westmorland into the eleventh century, and it may be that these tales are part of their heritage of folklore, adapted for more modern tastes. Gawain does not enjoy this position of unrivalled hero in the French romances, and it is difficult to account otherwise for his sudden pre-eminence here except by a particular local cult of his name.

Three other Gawain poems follow the more usual pattern of translation from French originals. The first, *Ywain and Gawain*, an early fourteenth-century poem from the north of England, is a direct translation of Chrétien de Troyes' masterpiece *Yvain*. The English work is a little over half the length of its original; Chrétien's introspective monologues, psychological digressions, and observations on love were not to the taste of the English, and the translator has condensed such passages in order to allow the plot to move forward more swiftly. However, he is far from ruthless in his excisions, sometimes merely exchanging indirect for direct speech, and there is a great deal more about motive and feeling than is usual in an English poem of this kind. His verse and style are forthright, and he manages this deliberate simplicity to good effect.

The Gest of Sir Gawain is a fifteenth-century version of an incident from the first of the two continuations of Chrétien's *Conte del Graal,* of which only a fragment survives. Gawain appears in an unfavourable light, even though the English poet has combined two separate episodes in the original to show him to better advantage. As the fragment begins, Gawain is making love to a lady, whose father arrives and find them lying together. Gawain is forced to fight him, and defeats him; his sons then attack Gawain in turn, but only the third, Brandelis, is a match for Gawain, and in this case the outcome is undecided. They agree to meet again, but the English poet, perhaps wearying of his task, cuts short the sequel in his original by saying:

And after that time they never met more
Full glad were those knights therefore.

This was a popular tale in Elizabethan times; a printed fragment survives, and licences to print it were granted to two printers in about 1580.

A Scottish work, drawn from the same French source, uses a similar technique in adapting the original, and dates from much the same period. *Golagros and Gawain* uses two unconnected incidents in order to glorify Gawain. In the first, Kay is used as a foil to Gawain, who makes amends by his courtesy for Kay's boorishness, while the second culminates in a duel between Golagros and Gawain in which Gawain's courage and generosity are emphasised. The details of the French romance, unflattering to Gawain, are altered to achieve the desired effect; battles replace tournaments and war takes precedence over love.

118

Archaic forms abound in the rather limited vocabulary, and the Scottish dialect is much in evidence. As so often with alliterative verse, the battle scenes are the strongest point of the work. There is a vigour and clarity often lacking in translations, as in this passage from Gawain's battle with Golagros:

> With ane bitand brand burly and braid
> Whilk oft in battale had been his bute and his belde
> He leit gird to the grome with greif that he had
> And claif throw the cantell of the clene schelde;
> Throw birny, and breist plait, and bordour it baid;
> The fulie of the fine gold fell in the feild.
> The rede blude with the rout folowit the blaid,
> For all the wedis, I wise, that the wy weild,
> Throw claspis of clene gold, and clowis sa clair,
> Thair with schir Golagros the sire
> In mekill anger and ire
> Alse ferse as the fire,
> Leit fle to his feir.[5]

With this we come to the end of the Gawain poems and of the English romances in general. Turning aside for a moment, it is interesting to review the progress of Gawain's character. From an unimportant role in the *History of the Kings of Britain*, he appears to rise rapidly in the French romances. But even in the first sources he is Arthur's nephew; and in certain societies a man's sister's son was regarded as more important than a son. So his position in the stories is perhaps assured from the first: he quickly becomes the first knight of Arthur's Court, skilled in knightly arts, courteous and gentle. But he was by no means perfect in the French romances, and as Lancelot rose to become the chief Arthurian hero, so Gawain's faults were dwelt on in proportion. It was the English writers who raised him to the standing of the perfect knight, and fashioned a masterpiece around him. By contrast, the French version of Arthur's downfall places a good deal of the blame for the disintegration of the Round Table on Gawain, and Malory, drawing on this, includes him among the 'murtherars of good knightes', a portrait redeemed by his moment of greatness in his last letter to Lancelot. Tennyson, ignoring earlier English tradition, depicts him as one of the worse elements in Arthur's Court, a sad ending for the great hero of medieval literature.

The English romances as a whole are no match for the Continental works about Arthur and his Court. A steady mediocrity, with occasional lapses into crudity, and only one major masterpiece, is the sum of their literary achievement. Yet they reflect the taste of a rather different audience which also enjoyed the Arthurian stories, and the plots that the English writers chose are much more coherent than their French and German counterparts. The diffusion of the English romances was much slighter than elsewhere, even when they were of considerable literary quality, and there are far fewer reworkings of the material, with the exception of the debased coinage of the ballads.

Like their Continental counterparts, the English Arthurian stories enjoyed a great vogue immediately after the introduction of printing; but the book that brought this about belongs to our next chapter. The ballads also continued to be read, printed and recited in Elizabethan times, and the early ballad collections, such as Percy's *Reliques*, contain a number of examples, drawn from Malory or the French romances. But we are in the land of Sir Bredbeddle and Sir Marramile, and the only originality shown is usually the result of corruption of a complex earlier version. Sir Bredbeddle is a distant descendant of the Green Knight, and with this passage from the sublime to the ridiculous, our survey of medieval Arthurian romance in England might well end. Yet before it finally passed, there was to appear one of the most masterly versions of the legends in any language, which was also one of the great works of English prose. It is largely due to Malory that the Arthurian tradition survived in England long after it had become a mere antiquarian curiosity elsewhere; the last flower of romance was also one of the finest.

8

The Flower of Chivalry

The French Vulgate Cycle, although it contained the entire story of
Arthur, was a vast and unwieldy work, and even in France itself
attempts were made to reduce it to a coherent form. The best of
these, made by Michel Gonnot for the book-loving Duc de Nemours,
Jacques d'Armagnac, was completed in 1470, but concentrated on
chivalric adventure rather than Arthur himself. It was only when Sir
Thomas Malory came to put the same material into English that a
coherent version in manageable form of the whole story of Arthur
and his knights was produced. Malory achieved this by retaining the
main features of the stories, while rejecting those unsuitable or over-
lengthy for the English taste. The translation alone was a formidable
task: indeed, only one other anonymous writer had attempted a similar work by producing an English *Prose Merlin*. But interest in a
complete version of the legend in English at this period is shown by
Henry Lovelich's amateur efforts in verse to render the Merlin and
Grail stories, which date from 1460–70. Just as it had been in the
prose versions that the French romances had attained their greatest
popularity, so it was in Malory's works – albeit in edited form – that
the romances reached their highest esteem in England.

Malory himself is an enigmatic figure. Four or possibly five men
bore the name Thomas Malory at the period when *Le Mort Darthur*
was written. Of these, only two are serious candidates. The first is the
man usually accepted as the author; but there are, as we shall see,
serious difficulties and objections. Sir Thomas Malory of Newbold
Revel in Warwickshire was born in about 1410. At the age of twenty-
three, he inherited the family estates, and in the following year may

121

have served at Calais under the Earl of Warwick, with one lancer and two archers. He married in about 1440, and had one son, who died within his father's lifetime. So far there is little problem; but at the age of about forty he embarked on what a biographer has called 'an orgy of lawlessness'. Between June 1450 and July 1451 he committed or was accused of a dozen crimes, including attempted murder, theft, rape and extortion. He was arrested and imprisoned at Coleshill in July 1451, but escaped within a day or two by swimming the moat. His recapture took place, after further robberies, in the following month, and he spent the next three years in prison, save for a brief interval in 1452. However, on his release on bail in May 1454, he continued his career of crime in Essex. In October of the same year he was imprisoned in Colchester Castle, and was unable to appear at the expiry of his bail. He was handed over to the Marshal in November, and we know nothing more until February 1456, when he produced a writ of pardon issued by the Duke of York during his period of office as Lord Protector in November 1455 in answer to the charges against him. The following month he borrowed a sum of money, and sat for his shire in Parliament. He apparently failed to repay the debt, for he was imprisoned in Ludgate until October 1457, when he was once more released on bail. At the end of two months he returned to prison. The date of his release is not certain, but in 1459 he was apparently at large in Warwickshire. In Lent 1460 he was recaptured and imprisoned in Newgate.

This was to be his last criminal imprisonment, and in 1462 he accompanied the Earl of Warwick on Edward IV's expedition to Northumberland, and was at Bamburgh and Alnwick (to which reference is made in *Le Mort Darthur*) during the sieges. There is reason to believe that he joined the Lancastrians when Warwick broke with Edward IV, and was active in the campaign against the latter, for he is excluded specifically from two general pardons to the Lancastrians granted in 1467. His final imprisonment in 1469–70 seems to have been for political reasons; it is this period that coincides with the production of *Le Mort Darthur*. Whether he was released before his death on 14 March 1471 we cannot tell, but he is buried not far from Newgate prison, in Greyfriars Church.

Such a turbulent career accords ill with the noble sentiments of the book to which the name of Sir Thomas Malory is attached; and a recent investigator, Professor William Matthews, has put forward an alternative and hitherto unnoticed candidate who seems to have strong claims. This is Thomas Malory of Hutton and Studley in Yorkshire, who, although never actually described as a knight, was certainly of sufficient standing for the title. Equally, he is not known to have been a prisoner, though in an age of frequent warfare there is no reason why he should not have been an honourable captive, and Matthews ingeniously suggests the possibility of his imprisonment in the Armagnac lands. Furthermore, the linguistic analysis of *Le Mort Darthur* reveals a knowledge and use of northern dialect rather than Warwickshire local turns of phrase; and there is a link between the Yorkshire Malory and a French manuscript of the *Merlin* on which *Le Mort Darthur* seems to have been based, and of which only this one copy is known. The use of the alliterative *Morte Arthure*, again in northern dialect and with a unique manuscript coming from Lincoln, would also be more plausible in the case of the Yorkshire Malory. It is also perfectly possible that the Malory referred to in connection with the sieges of Bamburgh and Alnwick and the pardon of 1467 was the Yorkshire candidate. The case for Sir Thomas Malory of Hutton and Studley as our author is a strong one, even if proof positive is lacking.

Scholars are equally divided about the exact intentions of the author of *Le Mort Darthur*. In its original version, it was divided into eight separate books. For some three and a half centuries, Caxton's edition of 1485, which welds them into one, albeit not very coherent, single composition, was regarded as being a more or less faithful reproduction of the original. In 1934, however, there came to light in the Winchester College Fellows' Library a unique manuscript of the eight tales, which for the first time revealed the earliest form of Malory's composition. But the question of whether Malory intended from the start to produce a complete cycle in separate parts, or whether he progressed by adding to his existing work until he reached the point where an attempt at completeness was almost inevitable, is still the subject of fierce debate. It is true that the chronology throughout the work is not continuous, and the tales were intended to have some degree of independence, perhaps dictated by the sources from which Malory worked. For example, the birth of Sir Tristram is related three hundred pages after his appearance, which argues a *prima facie* case for the independence of two of the books at least, as does the injunction at the end of the first book to 'seke other bookis of kynge Arthure or of sir Launcelot or sir Trystrams . . .' if the reader wishes to know more. The most reasonable solution seems to be that Malory did not intend to continue his task at this point; but when he changed his mind, he produced a work which conforms to medieval rather than modern ideas about logic and consistency of approach. After all, these are romances, not works of schoolmen or philosophers, and it would be foolish to expect an exacting regard for consistency from an author whose very subject is full of incidents which defy the rational order of things.

So we must reject both the unity praised by the earlier critics – 'of this vast assemblage of stories only Malory makes one story and one book' – and an absolute division between the tales. It is possible that the second tale, *The Tale of King Arthur and the Emperor Lucius* may be Malory's first literary effort, antedating even *The Tale of King Arthur* with its dismissive remarks implying that there was no more to come. *Arthur and Lucius* is an almost straightforward reworking in prose of the alliterative *Morte Arthure* already mentioned. This epic-heroic work had a great influence on his style, and there is virtually none of the reordering and recomposing found further on; the narrative of the poem is direct and uncomplicated, and needs no simplification. Some of the lines are quoted in full without alteration; and perhaps for this reason it was here that Caxton made his most considerable abbreviations; his version bears little resemblance to what Malory actually wrote.

In view of this close translation of the French, it is strange to find here another example of the insertion of contemporary references, parallel with those in Geoffrey of Monmouth and in the alliterative *Morte Arthure* itself. Malory does not go so far in this direction as his predecessors, of whose efforts at alteration he was in all probability unaware. Arthur is modelled in some respects on Henry v, as is suggested by his route through France, which is reminiscent of the campaign preceding Agincourt. Instead of Mordred, two chieftains are left as regents, in much the same way as Henry appointed Bedford and Beaufort. In addition, Arthur is actually crowned by the Pope, a parallel to Henry vi's French coronation. Otherwise, the only change of emphasis, to which we will return, is the new prominence given to Lancelot as a warrior-hero, who is given the role assigned to Gawain in the original. This may have been part of a later revision, when the character of Mordred and the closing scenes were also removed.

It seems likely that it was after this adaptation from an English poem that Malory turned his attention to the French romances. If Matthews' theory is correct, he borrowed from a neighbour in Yorkshire the version of the *Merlin* known as the Huth Merlin, which differs substantially from the *Estoire de Merlin* in the Vulgate Cycle, although it is perfectly compatible with the latter. On reading the French, he must have discovered very rapidly that a totally different story-telling technique was involved, as complex as that of the English poet had been direct and simple. A number of themes were interwoven in an almost inextricable mesh, giving a tapestry-like effect to the whole. Quite frequently, the themes or their sequels extended between separate romances, thus giving the Cycle its unity. Malory succeeded in both isolating many of the incidents, often told in passages many pages apart in the French, and in strengthening such links as remained, especially if they offered a point of contact between his own tales. This process is well illustrated by the *Tale of Balin and Balan*, where Malory has added to the original story the incident of the Dolorous Blow, by which an entire country is laid waste. The latter forms a quite separate incident in the original, but by adding it, Malory heightens the portrayal of Balin as a fated knight, who is destined to do harm. It is chiefly changes of this kind that distinguish *The Tale of King Arthur* from a mere translation, and which enable Malory to reduce the prominence of Morgan le Fay and Merlin, concentrating instead on Arthur himself.

Lancelot, as we have seen, first appears in the *Tale of King Arthur and the Emperor Lucius*, and this puts his story in a different light.

125

He now rises to fame by his military exploits in the Roman Wars, and goes on to become first knight of the Round Table in deeds of chivalry threafter, whereas the reverse was true in the French cycle. His position as Guinevere's lover, the role in which his character first became of importance, is given less emphasis by Malory, who did not entirely sympathise with the point of view of the French writers on this.

The Tale of Sir Lancelot du Lake falls into three sections. The first of these is the third part of the French *Lancelot*. Malory has reduced it by about a half, while retaining the outline of the original. He then moves to the next reference to the Lancelot-Lionel theme, separated by many pages of material on other themes in the French version, which he omits *en bloc*. The third section has no known source, but it is probable that Malory followed with the same degree of closeness a version of the romance now lost. The Chapel Perilous episode is similar to an incident in the French romance *Perlesvaus*, but it is unlikely that this is the direct original, since so much of the rest of the story in it is violently at odds with the Vulgate Cycle. The sections chosen from this unknown work deal entirely with adventures pure and simple, without any underlying theme. The conclusion, as so often, is Malory's own, and probably cuts short his source well before the end.

For *The Tale of Gareth* there is again no known source. The romance *Sir Libeaus Desconus* bears some resemblance to it, and an incident in the French *Prose Tristan* may have contributed to it. It was from this latter that Malory learnt of Gawain's evil reputation, and it is not until the last section of *Le Morte Darthur* that he regains his old character. *The Tale of Sir Gareth* is the shortest unit of Malory's works; the next, *The Book of Sir Tristram de Lyones* represents over one-third of his entire output, and is drawn from the same source, a version of the *Prose Tristan* which does not correspond exactly to any surviving manuscript. Here Malory begins to treat his material with increasing freedom and confidence. He firmly omits the whole of the third book of the original, which dealt with some of the Grail adventures, saying: 'Here endyth the secunde boke off syr Trystram de Lyones, whyche drawyn was oute of freynshe by sir Thomas Malleorre, knyght, as Jesu be hys helpe. Amen. But here ys no rehersall of the thirde booke.' The introduction dealing with Tristram's parentage has also been omitted, and the whole is divided into sections, each with an *incipit* and *explicit* in the Winchester manuscript.

Malory has not altered the literary style of the French so much as its character. The Tristram story is not presented here as a tragedy; we only learn of the death of the lovers – in a version very different from the earliest and most familiar one – by a chance remark in the last part of *Lancelot and Guinevere*. The tragic undertones disappear with the blackening of Mark's character, thus representing Iseult as in great measure justified in turning to Tristram. Tristram becomes above all a knight-errant; his love for Iseult seems to be less the prime motive of his existence than an adjunct of his chivalry. The return of the lovers to Joyous Gard is invented by Malory to replace the ending of the original, and we leave them in domestic bliss there. This replacement of earlier attitudes by his own brand of chivalry is typical of Malory; yet he fails to remove entirely Sir Dinadan, whose mocking counterpoint questions the very ideals he cherishes, in the manner of a privileged jester.

Some of Malory's sections are interpolations into the *Prose Tristan* from other sources, and it is interesting that despite his overall simplifications he accepts many of these episodes, such as the stories of Alexander the Orphan and the tournament at Surluse. These come from the fourteenth-century *Prophéties de Merlin*, while the story of Lancelot and Elaine is taken from the *Vulgate Lancelot*.

The original of the *Tale of the Sankgreall*, the French Vulgate *Quest for the Holy Grail*, follows the *Lancelot* section to form the fourth branch of the cycle. No surviving manuscript exactly corresponds to the passages selected by Malory, but there are no substantial differences in the actual material. His skill here has been directed at omissions calculated to alter considerably the character of the Quest. The French work was virtually an exposition of the doctrine of Grace and Salvation, and to emphasise and interpret the lesson of each adventure hermits appear on every other page, moralising or preaching over the unfortunate knights whose injuries they tend. Malory ruthlessly excises most of these, and abbreviates the moralisings of the surviving hermits. In doing so, he manages to make Lancelot, and the chivalry which Lancelot represents, emerge with much greater credit from the Grail adventures. He seems to have been concerned to diminish the distinction between religious and secular chivalry, and to remove the religious atmosphere of purification and repentance as a keynote of the Quest. Lancelot's relative success is emphasised rather than his eventual failure at the vital stage. If the result is not always sound theology, it brings the story more into line with the rest of the cycle.

For the last two of his eight tales, Malory combined English and French romances, but depended less and less on his sources. The two works he used were the rhyming *Le Mort Arthur* and the conclusion of the Vulgate Cycle, *La Mort Artu*. In the *Book of Sir Launcelot and Queen Guinevere*, the first two parts are careful selections taken almost directly from the sources. Thereafter he departs from any known version of either French or English. In *The Great Tournament*, for example, the actual description of the tournament is Malory's own work, and *The Knight of the Cart* is very much rewritten: whereas Chrétien long ago had made Lancelot's journey in the cart so shameful that Guinevere seemed almost divine in her power over him, Malory passes it over as merely another adventure. In *The Healing of Sir Urry*, he presents his own contribution to the legend, the apotheosis of Lancelot. After a vast procession of knights, whose names read like a roll-call of Malory's by now extensive reading, have failed to heal the stricken Sir Urry, Lancelot succeeds, and, movingly, weeps 'as he had bene a chylde that had bene beatyn' when this private miracle is granted him.

Until now, in spite of *The Tale of the Sankgreall*, Malory had had relatively little difficulty in making Lancelot his hero. But when he came to the tragic conclusion of the cycle, he found that the French writers had made Lancelot the main agent of Arthur's downfall. Malory could not blame him for this without bringing down the whole carefully-constructed edifice built around the idea of Lancelot as the flower of chivalry; nor did the blunt statement at the end of the previous tale actually resolve the problem: 'and now I go unto the morte Arthur, and that caused sir Aggravayne'. He had to make a

est chi ensi comment. lans cheuauoit par mi une foriest 7 il uinren
praerie. Er comment il carola ale carole ki estoit faite par enfante
r. Er comment il akieua chelle auenture 7 gmer on la sire une eriere

XVII–XXIII Illustrations from an early fourteenth-century manuscript of the adventures of Lancelot.

XVII *Above:* Lancelot breaks the spell on the dancers who are bewitched into dancing all the time until the best knight in the world shall come to release them.

XVIII *Left:* Lancelot forces a knight, who has cut off a lady's head because she has deceived him, to go to make amends at the court of King Baudemagus.

XIX Arthur and his court at a feast on the eve of Whitsun. This was the occasion on which the Grail appeared at the court, and the Grail quest began

XX Guinevere, condemned to be burnt at the stake for her adultery with Lancelot, is rescued by him and his companions in defiance of Arthur. After this, the Round Table fellowship is broken up, and the tragedy begins.

XXI Arthur and his court listen to a messenger from one of the knights on the Grail quest.

XXII Galahad fighting in a tournament.

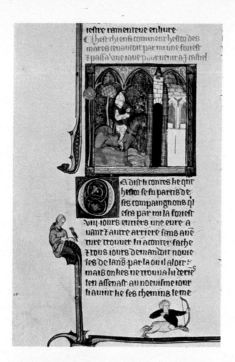

XXIII A knight errant on his adventures: Ector de Maris, Lancelot's half-brother, approaches a castle.

XXIV The Round Table which hangs in the great hall of Winchester Castle. It is believed to be of fourteenth-century date, but was repainted in the Tudor period.

XXV *Sir Galahad*, by
G. F. Watts. The model
for Galahad was the
actress Ellen Terry, to
whom Watts was briefly
and unhappily married.

XVI *The Lady of Shalott*, by William Holman Hunt. The basis of the picture is Tennyson's poem of the same name.

XXVII *Sir Galahad*, by Arthur Hughes. Galahad is shown on the Grail quest in a much more religious atmospher than Watts' version (see plate xxv).

XXVIII *The Quest for the Holy Grail:* a tapestry by William Morris and Co., from a design by Sir Edward Burne-Jon

Morgan le Fay, by Arthur Sandys. Morgan le Fay was Arthur's half-sister, and used her enchantments to try to destroy the Round Table and its knights.

xxx   *The Death of Arthur* by J. G. Archer. Arthur is shown supported by the three queens who have come t̶
take him to Avalon.

major alteration to the emphasis of the old tale, and he effected this by standing back from all moral judgements, thus shifting the focus onto character and situation rather than cause and effect. The feeling throughout this last book is that of a series of accidents, combined with regret and longing for what might have been. By heightening the intimacy of the relationship between Lancelot, Guinevere, Arthur and Gawain, the tragedy is intensified. Loyalty plays an important part: Lancelot's loyalty to Guinevere is brought into implacable opposition to Gawain's loyalty to kith and kin.

The conclusion is the most brilliant part of the work. The author of *La Mort Artu* became over-florid and the English poet insipid when confronted with this problem; but it is here that Malory's prose reaches its majestic climax of greatness and grief. His revision of the incidents of the last stages of the disaster is done with much finesse and feeling, especially where Lancelot's death is concerned. The French version makes him die, rather uncharacteristically, of religious devotion; but Malory gives the cause as his enduring love for Guinevere. A certain premonition of disaster before the great battle between Arthur and Mordred heightens the tension, while the aftermath show the totality and human intensity of the tragedy.

Throughout the later books, Malory's growing mastery over his material is evident. Earlier writers had been concerned with meanings as well as events, a trait seen at its worst in the French *Quest for the Holy Grail*. The romances became either fantasies irrelevant to real life or moral illustrations, and both abound in earlier Arthurian literature. Malory achieves a reality that requires no moral standpoint as its excuse or purpose, and has turned to the interplay of character and situation instead. Yet this absence of moral does not mean that he has no hero, but that his hero is all too fallible. And this also works in reverse; for he does not seem to have set out with the conscious intention of writing a story without a moral standpoint. He arrived at his effect by a process of evolution. It would be no great exaggeration to say that, having chosen Lancelot as his ideal, he altered everything to harmonise with this, and to show him in a better light where necessary. Hence it is chivalry rather than courtly love in which his practical nature is interested, and he does his best to divorce the two. This led him into major difficulties, for in the French romances the two are quite inseparable. Lancelot is challenged by a damsel whom he has just rescued, who says: 'But one thyng, sir Knyght, methynkes ye lak, ye that ar a knyght wyveles, that ye woll not love som mayden other jantylwoman' and repeats the rumour that he loves Guinevere. Lancelot instead of protesting his single-minded adoration of his lady, defends himself on quite different grounds:

> For to be a weddyd man, I thynke hit nat, for that I muste couche with hir and leve armys and turnamentis, battellys and adventures. And as for to sey to take my pleasaunce with peramours, that woll I refuse: in prencipall for drede of God, for knyghtes that bene adventures sholde nat be advoutrers nothir lecherous, for than they be nat happy nother fortunate unto the werrys; for other they shall be overcom with a sympler knyght than they be hemself, other ellys they shall sle by unhappe and hir cursednesse bettir men than they be hemself. And so who that usyth peramours shall be unhappy, and all thynge unhappy that is about them.

Knighthood is a vocation from which there is no respite, and love has become an obstacle on the knight's road, as Iseult points out when Tristram refuses to go without her to Arthur's Court: 'For what shall be sayde of you amonge all knyghtes? "A! se how Sir Trystram huntyth and hawkyth and cowryth within a castell wyth hys lady, and forsakyth us. Alas!" shall som sey "hyt ys pyté that ever he was knight, or ever he shulde have the love of a lady" '. The High Order of Knighthood is the great theme of Malory, and its code his ideal; knighthood can only survive as long as it remains the supreme ideal. Once the knights put their personal feelings before all else, the darkness of tragedy descends. Indeed, it is arguable that the decline begins with the overthrow of Lancelot by his son Galahad in *The Tale of the Sankgreall*. In the light of the earlier part of the work, this reverse seems scarcely credible, and Lancelot himself is stunned by it. But Malory does not transfer the central place to Galahad. His code of knighthood has become involved with forces above it and beyond it; and he merely accepts the moral offered by the French author and continues on his own path, putting the earthly worship attached to the Grail quest before its religious and spiritual benefit. His lack of enthusiasm for Galahad and Perceval is noteworthy and springs from the same cause as his rejection of the legacy of *amour courtois*: he prefers the practical to the ethereal and spiritual.

Malory's preference for Lancelot is underlined by his account of Lancelot's deeds in the quest for the Grail. In the French original, Lancelot's unworthiness and failure is emphasised, while Malory stresses his partial success in achieving the vision of the covered Grail at Carbonek. Malory accuses Lancelot only of instability, but does not specify his sinfulness more explicitly. And the grave and noble pages which tell of the achievement of the Quest belong to a separate world, where secular knighthood still has its representatives in the nine knights of Gaul, Ireland and Denmark, and in Sir Bors; but as Sir Bors returns to Camelot from Sarras, bearing Galahad's greeting to the Court, we feel that it is the Round Table above all else that has made this achievement possible. In Arthur's command that 'grete clerkes ... shulde cronycle of the hyghe adventures of the good knyghtes' earthly worship is once again to the fore.

But the ultimate effect of the Grail story is to produce a hero who is fallible, an important step towards the modern novel; for Lancelot is still the hero after his failure. Malory might have preferred to make Arthur his hero, but the French stories did not provide enough material on which to build his reputation. As it is, he is hero of the first two parts, and Malory pays him the highest compliment he knows: 'of him all knights may learn to be a knight'. Guinevere, like all Malory's female characters, lacks life and conviction; her main function in the French romances, to be Lancelot's lady and mistress, is played down, and Arthur's interest is concentrated on his company of knights rather than her. In the final stages of the tragedy he declares: 'And much more I am soryar for my good knyghtes losse than for the losse of my fayre quene; for quenys I myght have inow, but such a felyship of good knyghtes shall never be togydirs in no company.'

The remaining characters are chiefly the knights: Galahad and Perceval, the unearthly seekers after spiritual perfection, for whom Malory does not greatly care; the imitators of Lancelot, who cannot quite attain his level of knightly prowess; and the group of whom Gawain is the chief representative, meaning well but unfortunate in their actions. Gawain is a strongly drawn character: impetuous, quick to repent, courageous yet misguided and obstinate, he is in some ways more human and sympathetic than Lancelot, and his farewell letter to the latter is one of the most moving moments of the story. The magical characters, Merlin and Morgan le Fay, are reduced in stature by Malory, who has less time for the grotesque and incredible than his predecessors; and since Morgan le Fay's plots served largely to complicate the French romances, Malory's simplifications sweep away many of the episodes.

Malory's singleness of purpose in following out his chosen themes and characters is all the more remarkable when one turns to the French and observes how widely separated the component parts often are. This unravelling of the threads of the Vulgate Cycle and the gathering of them into simpler patterns must have been Malory's hardest won achievement; out of its diffuseness, recurrent themes and unwieldy branches, Malory forged a coherent whole, cutting away the multiplication of incidents that have no real value as far as his main plot is concerned, and drastically abbreviating the wordy disquisitions on love, religion and chivalry which had encumbered the story. The prose of the French was, like the frame of the work, an unwieldy tapestry. Out of this Malory drew phrases with a clear cadence. His prose is crisp, lucid and rhythmic, varying in tone with the events it describes, quick and fierce for a combat: 'So when Sir Launcelot saw his party go so to the warre, he thrange oute to the thyckyst with a bygge swerede in his honde. And there he smote downe on the ryght honde and on the lyffte honde, and pulled down knyghtes and russhed of helmys that all men had wondir that ever knyght myght do suche dedis of armis.' Or it can become elegiac and solemn in grief:

'And now I dare say, thou sir Launcelot, there thou lyest, that thou were never matched of erthely knyghtes hande. And thou were the curtest knkght that ever bare shelde! And thou were the truest frende to thy lovar that ever bestrade hors, and thou were the trewest lover of a synful man that ever loved woman and thou were the kyndest man that ever strake with swerde. And thou were the godelyest persone that ever cam emonge prees of knyghtes, and thou was the mekest man and the jentyllest that ever ete in halle emonge

132

ladyes, and thou were the sternest knyght to thy mortal foo that ever put spere in the reeste.'

Than there was wepyng and doloure out of measure.

Within the ponderous elaborations of the Vulgate Cycle, there lay hidden a great epic drama, ranging through every human passion, joy and grief. Malory drew out the noble tragedy of Arthur from the mass of adventures and marvels in which it had become entangled, and gave to it a new unity and clarity. He made its protagonists real people once more, stripped off the moralising to restore the unrelenting onset of the tragedy, and gave to the climax a befitting majesty and grandeur which it had never before attained. It needed Malory's skilful hand to reveal the full force of the 'noble chyvalrye, curtosye, humanyte, frendlynesse, hardynesse, love, frenlshyp, cowardyse, murder, hate, vertue and synne' which in Caxton's words the epic contained. By doing so he ensured that the Arthurian tradition, at least in England, did not become a mere literary curiosity like the medieval stories of Charlemagne and Alexander, but would re-emerge to inspire new masterpieces.

9

An Enduring Fame

Within a few years of the completion of *de Mort Darthur*, it seemed that a real King Arthur might soon rule in England. The accession of Henry VII, proud of his deeply-rooted Welsh ancestry, brought to the throne a dynasty whose promise of a better order of things combined with a vigorous nationalist policy was symbolised in their political propaganda by the revival of the idea of the 'return of Arthur'. The eldest son of Henry VII was christened Arthur, and was created Prince of Wales in November 1489, an event duly celebrated by John Skelton and the Court poets. And despite his untimely death in 1502, the Arthurian theme continued to play a large part in the mythology of the Tudor dynasty. Manuscript genealogies from Elizabeth's reign trace her lineage back to Arthur, and that strange magus Dr John Dee reported in 1580 on 'Her Majesties Title Royall, to many forrain Countries, kingdomes and provinces by good testimony and sufficient proofs recorded', based on the Arthurian stories in the *History of the Kings of Britain*; Elizabeth received the document with approval, though Burghley, as usual rational and cautious, took a dim view of such imperial ambitions. Perhaps influenced by his acquaintance with Dee, Richard Hakluyt began his *Principal Navigations of the English Nation* with an account of Arthur's northern conquests.

Tudor royal pageants were often constructed around the theme of the Nine Worthies, a popular subject inherited from medieval writers. Three classical, three pagan and three Christian heroes made up the nine, Arthur being the first of three Christian worthies, followed by Charlemagne and Godfrey of Bouillon, King of Jerusalem.

Arthur appears at pageants at Coventry in 1498; at the marriage of Margaret Tudor and James IV of Scotland in 1503; at the Field of the Cloth of Gold in 1520; and in London processions of 1522 and 1554. At an entertainment for Elizabeth at Gray's Inn in 1587, a play modelled on Seneca, *The Misfortunes of Arthur* by Thomas Hughes was the piece chosen, with subject matter from Geoffrey of Monmouth. The tradition was continued under the Stuarts: an anagram current early in James' reign, and quoted by Camden and Ben Jonson, reflected popular hopes under another new dynasty, identifying the Arthur whom Scottish historians had so reviled with the Scottish king:

> Charles Iames Steuart
> Claimes Arthures seat

Ben Jonson, writing masques for James' elder son, Prince Henry; introduced Arthurian themes. In *Prince Henry's Barriers* of 1612, devised as framework for a tournament, Arthur appears in the guise of the star Arcturus to give his blessing to the proceedings; and the *Masque of Oberon*, in which Prince Henry played Oberon, pays homage to James as a second Arthur.

Meanwhile, Tudor antiquarians, encouraged to investigate Arthurian history by this royal use of the legend, were fighting out a bitter battle over his real character. Polydore Vergil, an Italian who spent some years in England on Papal business, was the first to attempt to question Geoffrey of Monmouth's wilder flights of fancy in his *Historia Anglica*, published in Basle in 1534. This was violently attacked by nationalist historians. John Leland, as King's Antiquary to Henry VIII, was almost duty bound to offer a defence to such passages as this in Polydore Vergil:

> As concerninge this noble prince, for the marvelus force of his boddie, and the invincible valiaunce of his minde, his posteritee hathe allmoste vaunted and divulged such gestes, as in our memorie emonge the Italiens are commonlie noysed of Roland, the nephew of Charles the Great bie his sister, allbeit hee perished in the floure of his yowthe; for the common people is at this presence soe affectioned, that with wonderus admiration they extol Arthure unto the heavens, alleginge that hee daunted three capitans of the Saxons in plain

135

feelde; that hee subdewed Scotlande with the Iles adjoyninge; that in the teritorie of the Parisiens he manfulie overthrew the Romaines, with there capitan Lucius; that hee did depopulat Fraunce; that finallie hee slewe giauntes, and appalled the hastes of sterne and warlike menne . . . . Not manie years since in the abbey of Galstonburie was extructed for Arthur a magnificent sepulchre, that the posteritee might gather how worthie he was of all monuments, whearas in the dayes of Arthure this abbaye was not builded.

Leland's riposte, the *Assertio Inclytissimi Arturii* (*Assertion of the Most Noble Arthur*) appeared in 1544, and depended on enthusiasm rather than any tangible evidence:

But here if ouer and besides this I should endevour largely, to adorne Arthure with praise as the multitude of Authours do most truly write and agree upon him; sooner should copy of eloquence faile, then magnificencie of lightsome testimony howsoever. Be it sufficient then that we use at this present the most famouse commendations, though of fewe writers. I pray you, what is the cause that Trittemeus in his breefe Crounicle maketh so excellent mention of Arthure. Doubtlesse the cause is plaine enough. For by reason he learned the same of others in plaine trouth, therefore did he as thankfull commit it unto posteritie which thing doubtlesse he would never have done, had he doubted of the veritie of the cause . . . .
What just occasion wish I here to be given me of Polidorus the Italian, that even by some memorable testimony of his, I might also advance Arthures countinance, and make him looke aloft? He handleth Arthures cause in deed, but by the way, he yet is so fainte harted, luke warme and so negligent that he makes me not onely to laugh, but also to be angry (as while he is contrary to truth, and filled with Italian bitternesse) I know not whether he smile or be angry. . . .

In the purely literary field, other romances than Malory's enjoyed a degree of popularity, the most important being Lord Berners' translation of a widely-read fifteenth-century French romance, *Arthur of Little Britain*, which appeared *c.* 1530. The translation itself does not approach that by the same author of *Huon of Bordeux*, but it is the plot which is of most interest to us. It is a fairy tale pure and simple, the story of a lover who beholds his beloved in a dream and seeks her human counterpart. Of this ethereal theme Arthur is the hero: and all pretence of reality disappears. It was not surprising that the Protestant moralists should attack the romances as part of the corrupt old order, and Roger Ascham put the case forcefully in his *Scholemaster*:

In our forefather's tyme, whan Papistrie, as a standynge poole, covered and overflowed all England, fewe bookes were read in our tong, savyng certaine bookes of chevalrie, as they said, for pastime and pleasure; which, as some say, were made in Monastries by idle monkes or wanton canons. As one, for example, *Morte Arthure*, the whole pleasure of which booke standeth in two speciall poyntes, in open mans slaughter and bold bawdrye. In which booke those be counted the noblest knightes, that do kill most men without any quarrell, and commit foulest advoulteries by subject shifties.

After such attacks, it is hardly surprising that the successors of *Arthur of Little Britain* are cast at a more popular level, such as Thomas Munday's translations of similar romances at the end of the sixteenth century. Two or three original works of slight merit appeared in the early seventeenth century, among them Richard Johnson's *Romance of Tom a Lincolne, the Red Rose Knight* of about 1610. It was a genre which soon descended even further to the level of popular chapbooks; those on Merlin were ridiculed *en passant* by Swift and Pope, but it was Fielding who demolished the romantic Arthur in *Tragedy of Tragedies or the Life and Death of Tom Thumb the Great*, a burlesque in which the diminutive hero is eventually devoured by 'the expanded jaws of a red-cow'.

More serious projects had meanwhile come to fruition, though even these are far removed from the medieval material on Arthur. First and foremost is Edmund Spenser's *The Faerie Queene* (1590). Spenser's starting point was the epic by Ariosto on the story of Roland, *Orlando Furioso*, tempered by the more sober example of another Italian working in the same epic vein, Torquato Tasso. Tasso had recommended Arthur as a suitable epic subject, while choosing the Crusades himself; and he had also echoed Aristotle's advice that the epic hero should embody one particular virtue. Spenser's choice, in view of the Italianate sympathies of the period, may well have been determined by this advice. Writing to Raleigh, he asserts:

> I labour to pourtraict in Arthure, before he was king, the image of a brave
> knight, perfected in the twelve morall virtues, as Aristotle has devised . . . .
> In the persone of prince Arthure I sette forth magnificence in particular, which
> vertue, for that (according to Aristotle and the rest) it is the perfection of all
> the rest, and conteineth in it them all, therefore in the whole course I mention
> the deedes of Arthure applyable to that vertue which I write of in that booke.

But *The Faerie Queene* borrows only the person of Arthur and some
few trappings from the world of romance. It is above all an allegory,
whose plot is dictated by the working out of a greater meaning, and
not a mere tale. Spenser's sources are once more the Italians, and the
whole concept owes much to the cult centred on Elizabeth herself as
Gloriana, whose knight Arthur is. The use of this or that detail from
romances, whether Malory, *Libeaus Desconus* or *Arthur of Little
Britain*, does not make it a piece of true Arthurian literature; rather,
following the fashion for Arthurian references in pageantry, Spenser
has borrowed the name Arthur for his character Magnificence. And
when the poet begins work, Arthur remains a shadowy figure beside
the more vivid portraits in the individual episodes. It is for these that
The Faerie Queene is remembered as poetry rather than the
grandiose and eventually uncompleted architecture by which they are
framed. And besides, because Magnificence partakes of all twelve
virtues, to each of which a separate knight is assigned, Arthur's function becomes that of a double, often superfluous, to the other heroes.
Yet his splendid appearance at the outset remains memorable:

> His haughtie helmet, horrid all with gold,
> Both glorious brightnesse, and great terrour bred;
> For all the crest a Dragon did enfold
> With greedie pawes, and over all did spred
> His golden wings; his dreadfull hideous hed.
> Close couched on the bever, seem'd to throw
> From flaming mouth bright sparkles fierie red,
> That suddeine horror to faint harts did show,
> And scaly tayle was stretcht adowne his backe full low.

The Faerie Queene was the only Arthurian project by a major
writer to come to fruition during the sixteenth to eighteenth cen-

turies. Milton considered an Arthurian epic, and it played an important part in the process of arriving at his final theme, *Paradise Lost*. Though there are only two definite references to his intention of writing this work, in *To Manso* and *Epitaphium Damonis*, his interest seems to have been keen for some time. But it was certainly never more than a project, and he later grew sceptical of the legends. In his *British History*, he questions the very existence of Arthur, and pours scorn on the stories told about him, as though on closer examination he had found that the subject lacked a firm basis and was therefore not suited to his great work.

Another project not fulfilled in its original form was that mentioned by John Dryden in the preface to his translation of Juvenal. He states his intention of giving up his dramatic work in order to write an Arthurian epic. Financial circumstances forced him to continue to write the more profitable plays, but his idea eventually took shape as a dramatic opera in collaboration with Purcell, *King Arthur*. The first version had a political bias in support of Charles II, but since production was delayed until 1691, substantial alterations had to be made. In the process most of the central part of the work was cut out, and its final form is a very free version of Arthur's struggle against the Saxons, treated in the same fairy-tale manner as his adaptation of *The Tempest* four years later. Enchantments play a large part in the rather strained plot, entirely of Dryden's invention. It is Purcell's music which has given the work a continuing life.

One Arthurian epic, however, did see the light of day; it came from the pen of a minor writer, Sir Richard Blackmore, Physician in Ordinary to William III. Blackmore took up the writing of epics as 'an innocent amusement to entertain me in such leisure hours as were usually past away before in Conversation and unprofitable telling and hearing of News'. He studied the efforts of previous epic writers and the rules they followed, and set out to rival Homer and Virgil with his 'innocent amusement'. The results, needless to say, were hardly immortal. *Prince Arthur* (1695) and *King Arthur* (1697) are entirely modelled on earlier works. The contest of Raphael and Satan which recurs throughout is borrowed from Milton, much of the heroic adventure derives from Homer and Virgil, while political allegory plays a considerable part. Although Blackmore achieved great popularity in his own day, his reputation did not last long. Several contemporary satires were aimed at him, including Pope's *Martin Scriblerus*, in which Blackmore appears as Bathos, and these were sufficient to destroy his undeserved fame.

The early eighteenth century, ruled by a triumphant classicism, marks the lowest ebb of Arthur's fortunes. While historians were gradually coming round to a view of the historical Arthur not far from that held today – if a little over-confident about dates and places – writers pursued very different themes. It was only in about 1760 that any real interest was taken in the poetic versions of the Arthurian legend, a development which was part of a general revival of the study of medieval literature in the wake of the reaction against an excessively narrow interpretation of classical rules. Throughout Europe, the medieval poems were read and printed again for the first time in two centuries; and the earlier pieces, which we now regard as the most masterly versions, appeared in print for the first time, to be appreciated at their true worth as a result. In France the enthusiasm was relatively brief, and the effect on contemporary literature slight, though the works of men like La Curne de Sainte Palaye enjoyed a wide vogue. All too often the popularisations were in the vein of the Comte de la Vergue de Tressan's description of the love of Tristram and Iseult, which quite reduces it to an eighteenth-century pastoral flirtation or a gentleman entertaining his mistress after the theatre: 'We will refrain from mentioning certain private suppers between the beautiful Guinevere, Lancelot, and these two lovers [Tristram and Iseult]; and what delightful suppers they were!' Similar compilations from the old romances adapted to modern tastes were made throughout the nineteenth century, but the only serious contributions came from the historians rather than the creators of literature. Paulin Paris' edition of *Les romans de la Table Ronde* (1868 onwards) and Joseph Bédier's masterly reconstruction of the early version of *Le Roman de Tristan et Iseut* (1902 onwards) stand out as of more than specialist interest.

In Germany, a parallel revival augured better at the outset, when in the 1770s Christoph Wieland produced two adequate renderings of Arthurian tales; but thereafter the German Romantics preferred a medieval world drawn from their own imagination, surpassing in fantasy even the wildest of the earlier romances. Such works as did appear were concerned with the Tristan legend, harking back to Gottfried von Strassburg, with the exception of Karl Immermann's *Merlin* (1832) which makes the magician into a second Faust, though with little of the power of Goethe's great conception. But the work of German scholars did bear literary fruit: without their modern versions of Gottfried von Strassburg and Wolfram von Eschenbach, it would have been almost impossible for Richard Wagner to have chosen these Arthurian themes for his operas.

Wagner had read widely in medieval literature while he was living at Dresden, and had come across Kurtz's translation of Gottfried, which provided an ending to the unfinished original. Though the earliest references to a projected opera on the subject imply that it was to be undertaken only on the completion of the *Ring of the Nibelungs*, which also owes its subject to medieval poetry, Wagner again took up the subject when in difficulties over the composition of the *Ring* early in 1857, and *Tristan und Isolde* was completed in August 1859. Gottfried's poem, though simple enough in its powerful and tragic outline, required further simplification for dramatic purposes. Wagner reduces the action to the bare essentials: the first act deals with the love-potion, the second with the betrayal of the lovers, the third with their death. It is obviously impossible to discuss the opera in terms of its libretto only; as Ernest Newman wisely says, Wagner relies 'at least as much on music as on words to tell us who and what his characters are and what they feel at a given moment'. But it is fair to comment that in the resultant blend of words and music, the legend achieves an intensity which no modern poetry alone has matched. For Tristan and Isolde, even in the earliest versions of the legend, are conceived as being not quite of this world; they are bewitched, enchanted or possessed, and what they do is less important than what they feel. Hence music, with its direct appeal to the emotions, is arguably a more effective medium for an extended version of their story than poetry alone, which cannot sustain the lyrical mood of their love for more than a brief passage. Equally, the early versions of the legend can move us by their simplicity, a simplicity which rings false in the work of a modern writer. Where Wagner is on dangerous ground is in his handling of the themes of day and night, life-wish and death-wish; but the literal death-wish which dominates some parts of the opera is also a longing for the annihilation of self in the ecstasy of love, a concept entirely apt to the ancient tragic tale.

His treatment of the Grail legend has also been attacked on philosophical grounds. *Parsifal* was his last opera, completed in 1882. But the subject had attracted him for many years, and the first concrete mention of it is in an early sketch for *Tristan and Isolde* of 1854–5, where Parsifal was to appear as a pilgrim in the last act, as the archetype of a similar kind of eternal longing to that which haunted Tristan. Wagner had read both Simrock's and San Marte's renderings of Wolfram in 1845; and the idea was to take many more years to mature. He found it difficult to achieve the simple outline and logical action which is a feature of all his later operas: just as the driving force in *Tristan* is passion, so the inconsequences of the *Conte del Graal* and Wolfram's *Parzival* had to be reduced to the theme of redemption. In 1857 the idea of the Good Friday scene had taken shape, and in 1865 he had found the key: the mysterious spear of the Grail procession, cause of Amfortas' wound, became the spear with which Longinus had wounded our Lord at the Passion, an idea not to be found in Wolfram but borrowed from the French Vulgate Cycle. Here too he found the identification of the Grail as the cup used at the Last Supper, and the remaining details, such as Kundry's role as the temptress, fell into place. The idea of the Grail brotherhood seems to have been derived from the Knights Templars; it is foreign to the medieval romances.

Parsifal is probably the most controversial of Wagner's operas, and has been misread as a kind of Aryan brotherhood in embryo, or as the despairing repentance of an elderly lover of pleasure. In reality it is neither, nor is it specifically Christian. It is about redemption, certainly; but redemption is seen as a form of man's longing for the eternal, that same longing which in *Tristan und Isolde* was a desire to perpetuate love. Where Wagner's structure is at its weakest is in the motivation of Parsifal's redemption. Kundry is largely the composer's own creation. In the original she is a mere messenger, who begins Parzival's journey back to the Grail castle by her reproaches to him before Arthur's assembled knights. But in Wolfram, Parzival's wisdom is gained through plumbing the depths of spiritual despair, the moment when he curses God for not rewarding his faithful service. Wagner, probably for dramatic reasons, but perhaps also from his own psychological motives, makes the experience of Kundry's kiss, sensual experience, the trigger of despair and eventual redemption. Instead of the reconciliation of man's 'twy-nature' in Wolfram, Wagner chooses to play the ascetic; but he does not entirely convince us.

The mainstream of modern Arthurian literature, probably due to Malory, has been in English. Although Malory's book, the only complete version of the legends easily accessible to modern readers in any language, did not reappear in print until 1816, a similar antiquarian movement to that on the Continent had already brought about an Arthurian revival. Bishop Percy, in *Reliques of Ancient English Poetry*, published in 1765, included six Arthurian ballads, and drew attention to many of the romances in a list of his own compilation. Thomas Warton's *History of English Poetry* contained much general matter on the romances and his own poems include only two Arthurian ones from the eighteenth century. Within a short while editions of the romances proper appeared. Joseph Ritson, whose *Ancient English Metrical Romances* was published in 1802, was one of the more aggressive of the editors. He attacked Percy violently for being inaccurate in his reproduction of the originals, and tried to follow the manuscripts fastidiously in his own edition. Ritson's work was followed by Walter Scott's edition of *Sir Tristrem*, Robert Southey's *Malory*, and Sir Frederick Madden's *Syr Gawayne*, which collected the majority of the English Gawain poems for the first time.

Walter Scott's work is somewhat marred by an excessive admiration for the poet who wrote *Sir Tristrem*, who was no great genius and certainly not the Thomas of Britain who was then believed to have originated the Tristan and Iseult legend, as Scott so stubbornly maintained. This judgement led him, owing to the importance of the work, to provide his own completion in imitation of the original, which, as such, is very successful. Scott betrays his attitude to scholarly problems in a letter written shortly before the poem's publication: 'I am determined not only that my Thomas *shall* be author of *Tristrem*, but also of *Hornchild*.'

This partisanship in favour of Thomas of Ercildoune appears all the more extraordinary when considering Scott's display of a fairly considerable knowledge of Arthurian literature in his one original effort in the field. But his information came chiefly from the French, and he seems to have been ill acquainted with the English contemporaries of Thomas. *The Bridal of Triermain* appeared in the *Edinburgh Review* of 1809 anonymously, and for some time Scott refused to acknowledge it, but he eventually relented and it is included in his *Collected Works*. The Arthurian material provides little more than a framework for a reworking of the Sleeping Beauty folk tale. Scott's main source is revealed by his treatment of the characters, which patently derive from French romance: Lancelot and Guinevere are openly lovers. There are also references to poems in Percy's *Reliques*. The plot is of no great interest, but there is the occasional set-piece in Scott's most gothic manner:

> Now caracoll'd the steeds in air,
> Now plumes and pennons wanton'd fair,
> But soon too earnest grew the game,
> The spears drew blood, the swords struck flame,
> And, horse and man, to ground there came
> Knights, who shall rise no more!
> Gone was the pride that war had graced,
> Gay shields were cleft, and crests defaced,
> And steel coats riven, and helms unbraced,
> And pennons stream'd with gore.

If Scott's approach was individualistic, that of Thomas Love Peacock was almost eccentric, though some of the strangeness is due to his use of genuine early Welsh tradition. This was to become more widely known after Lady Charlotte Guest published her translation of the *Mabinogion* in 1838; but his novel *The Misfortunes of Elphin* was written ten years earlier than this. Taliessin appears as Arthur's Court poet as, later, in the poems of Charles Williams), and as mediator between him and Melwas, king of the Summer Country, who carries off Guinevere; which last episode is taken from the eleventh-century *Life of St Gildas* of Caradoc of Llancarfan.

The whole of Peacock's work has a light and satirical tone; but this disguises a considerable knowledge of his material. He seems to have read much of the available Welsh literature in the original, and several of the poems are translations from the Welsh, though the well-known *War Songs of Dinas Vawr* is his own work. Arthur appears only infrequently, but the book is an amusing alternative to the rather pompous picture of the Arthurian Court presented by later Victorian writers.

Another writer who went back to early and unfamiliar sources was Bulwer Lytton, whose *King Arthur* (1848) draws on classical and Norse mythology as well. Arthur is set three tasks in order to win his kingdom, which include the gaining of Excalibur, the winning of the silver shield of Thor and visiting the Fates, as Perseus visited the Graiae in Greek legend. Some of the episodes come from the Gawain poems recently published by Sir Frederick Madden under the title *Syr Gawayne* (1839), while others are borrowed from French romance. The work as a whole, though much admired in the Victorian period, is uneven, the verse is trite and the humour forced. A modern reader is unlikely to agree with the artist Daniel Maclise who, having just finished work on two illustrations to Tennyson's *Morte D'Arthur*, exclaimed of Lytton's book: 'And oh what a book of subjects would the Lay of Arthur furnish . . .!'

The story of Tristram and Iseult was to be one of the most popular subjects in English poetry over the next fifty years, in part due to the influence of Wagner. The first complete modern version was that of Matthew Arnold in 1852, the first retelling for some five hundred years. His sources were chiefly French, with some details from Malory. Two articles by La Villemarque in the *Revue de Paris* (1837) which summarised the legend, and a similar abbreviation in Dunlop's *History of Prose Fiction* (1842) provided him with the main outline of the story, although he handled the material with some degree of freedom. Tristram, tended on his deathbed by Iseult of Brittany, waits for Iseult of Ireland to arrive. Here, unlike the original version, she comes in time to speak to Tristram before he dies, and their conversation is a series of memories of the past in which the whole story is relived. Tristram dies, and Iseult of Ireland expires on his bier. Iseult of Brittany is left to care for Tristram's children (again a departure from the original, where she is his wife in name only), and the poet describes her as she sits alone of an evening:

> ... and then
> She'll light her silver lamp, which fishermen
> Dragging their nets through the rough waves, afar,
> Along this iron coast, know like a star,
> And take her broidery-frame, and there she'll sit,
> Hour after hour, her gold curls sweeping it;
> Lifting her soft-bent head only to mind
> Her children, or to listen to the wind.
> And when the clock peals midnight, she will move
> Her work away, and let her fingers rove
> Across the shaggy brows of Tristram's hound
> Who lies, guarding her feet, along the ground;
> Or else she will fall musing, her blue eyes
> Fix'd, her slight hands clasp'd on her lap; then rise
> And at her prie-dieu kneel, until she have told
> The rosary beads of ebony tipp'd with gold;
> Then to her soft sleep — and tomorrow'll be
> Today's exact repeated effigy.

Arnold seems to prefer this vein of nostalgia, and a kind of domestic medievalism, to the high passion of Gottfried von Strassburg. He unfolds the story in a series of remembered scenes, denying himself immediacy for the sake of a broader, more evocative approach. Nor does he explore his characters' motives in any depth, and the wellsprings of Tristram and Iseult's love are never obvious. For it is Iseult of Brittany who emerges as the real heroine; the analysis of her feelings is finely executed, as are lesser details, such as the passage describing Tristram's children asleep while the lovers talk. Mood and atmosphere prevail over plot to the extent that the poem ends on a dying fall, with Iseult of Brittany telling her children how Vivien enchanted Merlin into an eternal sleep, 'for she was passing weary of his love'. Perhaps the poem is best seen as a study of modes of love: passion, tenderness, and, in this last episode, obsession.

We now come to the series of poems, which, after Malory, comprise the best known English version of the whole Arthurian legend. They are difficult to judge without prejudice, for the reaction against Victorian morals and ideals is not yet complete, and if any one writer embodies all their merits and faults, it is surely Alfred Lord Tennyson.

Tennyson's earliest sketch for a work based on the Arthurian legend dates from 1833, the year of the publication of his first independent collection of poetry. He conceived of the treatment as a single romantic epic, and sketched the opening of the work as follows:

> On the latest limits of the West in the Land of Lyonesse, where save the rocky isles of Scilly all is now wild sea, rose the sacred Mount of Camelot. It rose from the deeps with gardens and bowers and palaces, and at the top of the Mount was King Arthur's hall, and the holy Minster with the Cross of gold. Here dwelt the King in glory apart, while the Saxons whom he had overthrown in twelve battles ravaged the land, and ever came nearer and nearer.
>
> The Mount was the most beautiful in the world, sometimes green and fresh in the beam of morning, sometimes all one splendour, folded in the golden mists of the West. But all underneath it was hollow, and the mountain trembled when the seas rushed bellowing through the porphyry caves; and there ran a prophecy that the mountain and the city on some wild morning would topple into the abyss and be no more.
>
> It was night. The King sat in his Hall. Beside him sat the sumptuous Guinevere and about him were all his lords and knights of the Table Round. There they feasted, and when the feast was over, the bards sang to the King's glory.

Although the reviews of his second volume of poetry, published in 1842, deterred him from carrying out this plan, a second memorandum gives an outline of the underlying symbolism, traces of which were to persist in the finished version. King Arthur himself was to represent religious faith, and he was to have two wives, the first of whom was to be banished before he married the second, but later recalled. They were both to be called Guinevere,

147

echoing the theme of the true and false Guineveres found in Welsh legend; the first was to be the symbol of primitive Christianity, the second of Roman Catholicism. Mordred represented scepticism and Merlin science; Merlin's daughter was to wed Mordred. The Lady of the Lake, Nimue, stood for evil and corruption, a role which was little altered in the final version. Among the objects associated with Arthur, Excalibur stood for war, and the Round Table for 'liberal institutions'.

The next draft, some years later, is cast in a very different outward form, as a masque; but hints of the symbolism remain. Had Tennyson completed it, it would have been an original, though probably unsuccessful, contribution to Arthurian lore, with its own chronology and treatment of characters. The outline runs as follows:

FIRST ACT: Sir Mordred and his party. Mordred inveighs against the King and the Round Table. The knights, and the quest. Mordred scoffs at the Ladies of the Lake, doubts whether they are supernatural beings, etc. Mordred's cringing interview with Guinevere. Mordred and the Lady of the Lake. Arthur lands in Albyn.

SECOND ACT: Lancelot's embassy and Guinevere. The Lady of the Lake meets Arthur and endeavours to persuade him not to fight with Sir Mordred. Arthur will not be moved from his purpose. Lamentation of the Lady of the Lake. Elaine. Marriage of Arthur.

THIRD ACT: Oak tomb of Merlin. The song of Nimue. Sir Mordred comes to consult Merlin. Coming away meets Arthur. Their fierce dialogue. Arthur consults Sir Lancelot and Sir Bedivere. Arthur weeps over Merlin and is reproved by Nimue, who inveighs against Merlin. Arthur asks Merlin the issue of the battle. Merlin will not enlighten him. Nimue requests Arthur to question Merlin again. Merlin tells him he shall bear rule again, but that the Ladies of the Lake can return no more. Guinevere throws away the diamonds into the river. The Court and the dead Elaine.

FOURTH ACT: Discovery by Merlin and Nimue of Lancelot and Guinevere. Arthur and Guinevere's meeting and parting.

FIFTH ACT: The battle. Chorus of the Ladies of the Lake. The throwing away of Excalibur and departure of Arthur.

148

Tennyson did not decide finally on even the general shape of the cycle until some ten years later, in about 1855. Once he embarked on the project, work progressed rapidly, though *Balin and Balan* was not added until 1886. The outline of the cycle was complete in 1869, and an *Envoi* was added in1872.

Tennyson's reading in preparation for the work included much early Arthurian literature, though he depended heavily on Malory. There had been three editions of the *Morte Darthur* between 1816 and 1821, and it was now firmly entrenched as a classic work. He had read the *Mabinogion*, which Lady Guest translated in 1838, Layamon's *Brut* in Sir Frederick Madden's edition, and some of the French romances. He seems also to have made some study of the early Welsh material. He introduced few variations of his own, preferring to simplify Malory's many details, often with unfortunate results, as in his handling of the Tristram legend.

As the work progressed, Tennyson's concepts of the ideals underlying his stories seem to have changed and shifted somewhat, unlike Malory's resolute admiration for his chosen hero Lancelot. The symbolic element, too, occupied a less prominent place than originally intended, and was not intended to be interpreted as literally as the drafts might suggest. Tennyson said on one occasion: 'I hate to be tied down to say, "This means that", because the thought within the image is much more than any one interpretation.' Yet, on another occasion he provides a seemingly contradictory indication: 'Of course Camelot for instance ... is everywhere symbolic of the gradual growth of human beliefs and institutions, and of the spiritual development of man. Yet there is no single fact in the *Idylls*, however seemingly mystical, which cannot be explained without any mystery or allegory whatsoever.' His final judgement seems to have been this: 'Poetry is like shot-silk, with many glancing colours. Every reader must find his own interpretation according to his ability, and according to his sympathy with the poet.'

With these warnings in mind, there is nonetheless a broad general symbolism for us to discern. Arthur stands for the ideal soul. The whole epic is that of man's Utopian dreams coming into contact with practical life and the warring elements of the flesh, and how such high aspirations can be ruined by a single sin. Arthur's birth is a mystery, as is his death: 'from the great deep to the great deep he goes.' Between the two lies life with its conflict of flesh and spirit. He attempts to realise himself in the sensual world, represented by Guinevere, and to control and elevate human passion and capacity by 'liberal institutions', represented here, as in the earlier draft, by the Round Table. Thus Sir Galahad, who might at first seem to be the hero of the poems, is not in fact Tennyson's ideal: he is the figure of spiritual life divorced from this earth, who negates man's dual nature by withdrawing into purely spiritual realms. Merlin stands for the intellect, and his disastrous affair with Vivien is symbolic of the corruption of the intellectual by the sensual.

The keystone of Tennyson's cycle is therefore Arthur and the Table. Arthur himself appears as little short of perfect: warrior, statesman, the uniting force of the Round Table. Ambrosius says of his knights:

> Good ye are and bad, and like to coins,
> Some true, some light, but every one of you
> Stamp'd with the image of the King.

To follow and obey Arthur is the foremost law of the Round Table; and the high demands he makes are learnt by Gareth before he rides out to seek Camelot and Arthur's company:

> The King
> Will bind thee by such vows, as is a shame
> A man should not be bound by, yet the which
> No man can keep . . .

The vows that the King demands are clear and restrained, lacking the fire which knightly ardour might well desire; they accord well with Guinevere's first assessment of him as 'cold, high, self-contain'd, and passionless', though the description of the founding of the Order shows how Arthur himself could breathe enthusiasm into his warriors. Tennyson's code is dutiful rather than inspiring:

> To reverence the King, as if he were

Their conscience, and their conscience as their King,
To break the heathen and uphold the Christ,
To ride abroad redressing human wrongs,
To speak no slander, no, nor listen to it,
To honour his own word as if his God's,
To lead sweet lives in purest chastity,
To love one maiden only, cleave to her,
And worship her by years of noble deeds,
Until they won her.

It is in his match with Guinevere that Arthur fails. He misjudges
Lancelot, misjudges Guinevere, failing to see the other side of the
coin, the carnal passions which move him not at all. He chooses
Guinevere partly because only the most beautiful bride can match his
position and spiritual attainment, forgetting that earthly and
heavenly beauty are not one and the same thing. And from the high
hopes of the early poems, a steady progress towards the abyss of
failure develops. The sin of Lancelot and Guinevere permeates the
Court. Balin is unable to save himself because of the false ideals they
have spread; Pelleas and Etarre imitate their sin; the Holy Grail is
misunderstood and misused by the knights imbued with this worldly
ideal, of whom Lancelot is the chief, and they approach it with super-
stition instead of reverence. *The Last Tournament* shows the final
stage of the process, cynicism; this poem was originally entitled *The
True and the False* and sets the decay caused by the false ideal with
the original truth. Lancelot the bold has become slothful, Tristram
the courteous has forgotten his courtesy.

The cycle of poems is set at intervals throughout the natural
year: *The Coming of Arthur* on New Year's Day, his wedding 'when
the world is white with may', the appearance of the Grail at Camelot
on a summer's night. *The Last Tournament* is in the dead time of the
year, autumn, while the final battle in midwinter looks forward from
present disaster to the hope of the future rebirth and spring, through
Lancelot and Guinevere's repentance, and the forgiveness offered
them by Arthur.

Tennyson handles his material with varying degrees of freedom.
The Coming of Arthur is part of the allegorical scheme, and therefore
at variance with earlier versions; Arthur's antecedents are stripped

of their immoral medieval legend and shrouded in obscurity instead. *Gareth and Lynette*, *Balin and Balan* and *Merlin and Vivien* all depend on Malory, while the two Geraint poems go back to the *Mabinogion* romance also retold by Chrétien de Troyes in his *Erec et Enide*. A passage from *Lancelot and Elaine* shows how closely Tennyson could follow Malory on occasions:

> . . . lay the letter in my hand
> A little ere I die, and close the hand
> Upon it; I shall guard it even in death,
> And when the heat is gone out from my heart
> Then take the little bed on which I died
> For Lancelot's love, and deck it like the Queen's
> For richness, and me also like the Queen
> In all I have of rich, and lay me on it.
> And let there be prepared a chariot-bier
> To take me to the river, and a barge
> Be ready on the river, clothed in black.
> I go in state to court, to meet the Queen.
> There surely shall I speak for mine own self,
> And none of you can speak for me so well.
> And therefore let our dumb old man alone
> Go with me, he can steer and row, and he
> Will guide me to that palace, to the doors.

> And whyle my body ys hote lat thys lettir be put in my ryght honde, and my honde bounde faste to the letter untyll that I be colde. And lette me be put in a fayre bed with all the rychyste clothys that I have aboute me, and so lat my bed and all my rychyst clothis be ledde with me in a charyat unto the nexte place where the Temmys ys; and there lette me be put within a barget, and but one man with me, such as ye truste, to stirre me thidir; and that my barget he coverde with black samyte over and over.

In *The Holy Grail*, Tennyson treats Malory much as Malory had treated the French romances, extracting various incidents and welding them into a compact and unified narrative. Tennyson, as one would expect, takes a far more spiritual view than Malory, roundly condemning Lancelot; but he cannot entirely subscribe to the ideal of the Quest, which for him commits the cardinal error of isolating the

152

spirit from the flesh. His ideal remains that of Arthur, and Galahad triumphs only within his own limited sphere.

Tennyson now breaks away from the chronology of the *Morte Darthur* for his own purposes, introducing the story of Pelleas and Etarre from one of the earlier books, and uniting a series of separate incidents to form *The Last Tournament*. Here it is Tristram who comes in for harsh words; Tennyson has humbled both the great heroes of the medieval writers. In *Guinevere*, the Queen's retirement is moved back to precede Arthur's last battle, though the original plan had been for Arthur's speech at the end of the poem to round off the cycle (of which George Meredith said that Arthur lectured his Queen 'like a curate'). The adaptation of the *Morte D'Arthur* from the 1842 collection was Tennyson's final solution, adding 169 lines at the beginning, describing Arthur's dream and the actual battle, and 29 lines at the end which hark back to the line in *The Coming of Arthur*, 'From the great deep to the great deep he goes'.

It is hard for us today to recapture Tennyson's original impact, so debased has his noble idiom become through imitation and too frequent quotation. He is dealing in ideal and allegory rather than character, and his protagonists are often unconvincing. If he seems on occasions to lack real feeling, there is an atmosphere of high purpose in the tone of the poetry. This nobility falls easy prey to modern cynicism, as he himself foreshadowed in *The Last Tournament*, and we exalt passion and freedom over Tennyson's conservative chivalry and order. What we can admire is his craftsmanship as a poet, the many lovely descriptive passages – often in marked contrast to his moral attitude to the scene, as in Lancelot and Guinevere's first meeting in May – and the power with which he portrays the attraction of his ideals.

Just as it is the pictorial passages in Tennyson that speak to us most directly, so the most rewarding approach to the Victorian view of the Arthurian legend is often through the work of the Pre-Raphaelite painters and their successors. Tennyson and Malory were their chief inspiration, and the two most important painters to use Arthurian subjects were Sir Edward Burne-Jones and Dante Gabriel Rossetti, though Holman Hunt, Beardsley, Gustav Doré, and many lesser artists, such as James Archer and Henry Ryland, also contributed their visions of the medieval world. Two series of works stand out: the Oxford Union frescoes of the 1850s and Moxon's illustrated Tennyson of 1857. Sadly, the Oxford Union project was undertaken with an inadequate knowledge of the techniques of tempera painting, and many of the frescoes decayed very rapidly. It is chiefly in Burne-Jones' and Rossetti's water-colours that the freshness of the original inspiration survives.

William Morris, though he carried out several pictorial projects based on Arthurian legend, made a more important contribution through his poetry. He, like Tennyson, made early sketches for a full scale epic, but the four Arthurian poems included in his *Collected Works* are individual pictures, almost descriptions of works he never painted. *The Defence of Guenevere* is the Queen's speech defending herself at her trial. Too proud to deny the charges against her – 'Judge any way you will – what matters it?' – she longingly remembers Lancelot's love and care which had brought back the emotions of '. . . the time ere I was bought By Arthur's great name and his little love'. She rejects Sir Gawain's accusations hopelessly and defiantly, until at last the sound of Lancelot's rescuing charger brings joyous relief. In *King Arthur's Tomb*, Guenevere is torn between remorse and the sweetness of her memories. The power of the poem lies in its pictorial quality, and is closely linked to Rossetti's watercolour on the same theme. It uses in turn visual images to depict the Queen's state of mind:

And every morn I scarce could pray at all,
For Launcelot's red-golden hair would play,
Instead of sunlight, on the painted wall,
Mingled with dreams of what the priest did say; . . .

Morris sees more readily than most writers the failure and bitterness contained within the stories; Guenevere paying for her days of pleasure, Sir Bors describing (at the end of *Sir Galahad*) how:

The knights come foil'd from the great quest, in vain;
In vain they struggle for the vision fair.

and in *The Chapel in Lyonesse* the dying Sir Ozana le Cure Hardy declaring that 'my life went wrong' as he dreams of his love and:

> the tresses of her hair
> That shineth gloriously
>   Thinly outspread in the clear air
> Against the jasper sea.

Illustration by Aubrey Beardsley for *de Morte Darthur*

We are indeed deep in the world of the Pre-Raphaelites, of the pale beauties whose heavy-lidded eyes betray a yearning for past or future sweetness, the true Romantic *Sehnsucht*. If the proposed cycle would have been beyond Morris' capacity, he offers a powerful evocation of a single event or image; the briefer the poem, the surer his handling of it. His object was the realisation of a tragic event or situation, 'the perception and experience of tragic truth, of subtle and noble, terrible and piteous things'; and at his best he achieves almost visionary sight in the mood and setting of these rich pictures. Yet their weakness is that they are conceived in terms of another medium than poetry.

Morris' Arthurian poems are marginal to his fame: but the opposite is true of Algernon Swinburne. *Tristram of Lyonesse* was always intended to be his *magnum opus*, and is indeed the finest of the English versions of the subject. It covers most of the events of the traditional legend, though Swinburne overweights his material by attempting a sustained richness which the texture of the story will not always bear. Much reading preceded the composition of the poem; he studied the romances of Thomas and Béroul, insofar as they were published, as well as Scott's version of *Sir Tristrem* and Malory's excerpts from the French. The result is a story that rarely departs from the earliest form, save in the Palomides and Joyous Gard episodes, but which simplifies the outline of the tragedy by omitting detail.

Where Tennyson had debased Tristram and Iseult, fiercely condemning their love, Swinburne as fiercely glorifies them and their passion, exalting both while aware of the sinfulness inherent in the tale. His view is similar to, if more lenient than, that of Dante, who places them among the lesser sinners of the *Inferno*; their sin involves mutual sacrifice, but acknowledges no loyalty outside itself and thus leads the participants to betray others. Swinburne, like other writers, diminishes their guilt in this last respect by portraying Mark as mean and cold, until such time as he learns the truth and offers them noble forgiveness in death.

Swinburne obscures the story with psychological excursions, protracted similes and extended descriptions, as he attempts a continuous evocation of their feelings at each stage of the tragedy, from the amazement of their first fiery kiss through the woes of separation and joys of reunion, to the last moving scene where the lovers, who have seemed so young, are revealed as grown old and subject to death.

156

Through the poem run recurrent themes and motifs: the first and last embraces are connected by variations on the same words:

> Their heads neared, and their hands were drawn in one,
> And they saw dark, though still the unsunken sun
> Far through fine rain shot fire into the south;
> And their four lips became one burning mouth . . .
>   . . . and her head
> Bowed, as to reach the spring that slakes all drouth;
> And their four lips became one silent mouth.

Likewise, the ship that bears Tristram on the first fateful voyage is named *Swallow*, while that which takes Iseult on her last journey is called *Swan*. One theme runs throughout the whole poem, pervading it and occasionally dominating the verse: the sea itself. Both for the unknown author of the *Prose Tristan* and for Malory, Tristram had been a knight of the greenwood, a hunter skilled in venery. But for the earliest romancers who had formed and shaped the heart of the legend, Tristram was essentially a man of the sea. Swinburne harks back to this, and the theme provides a powerful and closely connected background against which to set his poem. *Iseult at Tintagel*, which shows Iseult in separation thinking of her distant lover, is continually underlined by the mood of the sea:

> And all their past came wailing in the wind,
> And all their future thundered in the sea.

The sea sets off and heightens the great moments of the tragedy. The famous love-potion is drunk against a background of storm; Tristram and Iseult both look seawards for comfort when they are parted; the lovelessness of Tristram's marriage to Iseult of the White Hands is emphasised by the sea's absence, and the one calm moment of their tempestuous relationship, at Joyous Gard, is mirrored in the sea's mood:

> Nor loved they life for death's sake less,
> Nor feared they death for love's or life's sake more

And on the sounding soft funereal shore
They, watching till the day should wholly die,
Saw the far sea sweep to the long grey sea.
And night made one sweet mist of moor and lea,
And only far off shore the foam gave light.
And life in them sank silent as the night.

The psychology of the lovers is skilfully drawn, as is Tristram's relationship with Iseult of Brittany; and the death scene is simply and tragically conceived. The jealous Iseult of Brittany, who has accidentally learnt of the prearranged signal, tells him that the sail is black, which means that her namesake of Ireland is not coming:

And fain he would have sprung upright and seen,
And spoken; but strong death struck sheer between . . .

Throughout the poem, there is more than an echo of Chrétien de Troyes and Gottfried von Strassburg, the two great medieval exponents of the literature of feeling. The psychological detail, the life-like portraits – as well as the secondary regard for narrative – all bring Swinburne's poem into the same class as the medieval writers.

Swinburne's other Arthurian work, *The Tale of Balen,* is more compact and direct. The theme of Fate, however, fails to work on his imagination as powerfully as the theme of love. The story, taken from Malory, is written in verse reminiscent of medieval stanzaic romance, just as *Tristram of Lyonesse* has affinities with the alliterative verse of the same period. Swinburne also echoes medieval nature-poetry in the opening of four of the cantos, and like *The Idylls of the King,* the action takes place within one natural year: Balen's youth is described against a background of spring, summer brings the height of his fame, autumn approaching doom and winter death.

Malory tells the story as pathetic rather than tragic, and makes of Balen's slaying of his brother an accident rather than a fore-ordained doom. Swinburne takes the latter view, making the tragedy arise from Balen's refusal to return a sword when asked to do so, a refusal which arises from his obstinate character; and it is this stubbornness which is the mainspring of the doomed and tragic tale. The abstract philosophising which mars parts of *Tristram of Lyonesse* gives way to a more direct and concrete imagery, though the overall effect is of a work in a lower and less compelling key.

After Tennyson's enormous success, a host of lesser writers seized eagerly upon the Arthurian stories. Little work of merit emerged, despite a wide diversity of treatment and subject. Direct imitation of Tennyson is rare; even R. S. Hawker, the Cornish antiquary whom Tennyson visited on one of his tours in search of Arthurian atmosphere, composed a *Quest of the Sangreal* which is surprisingly independent, drawing on Continental sources. Two other poets, the American J. R. Lowell and John Davidson, elaborated on the same theme in entirely idiosyncratic fashion: for Lowell, the Grail is a selfish quest, and his hero, Sir Launfal, achieves far more by homely works of charity. Davidson offers a secular view: Guinevere, as Lancelot's ideal, becomes his personal Grail and spiritual solace.

A number of playwrights undertook Arthurian stage works, but none of the dramatisations were particularly successful; one or two, based on Tennyson's own work, did have a temporary popularity in London, but even the librettos of Wagner's operas outshine by themselves any of the purely dramatic efforts. A distant descendant of the libretto for *Tristan and Isolde,* Arthur Symons' *Tristram and Iseult* (1917), offers the interesting view of Iseult as the dominant partner, seized by a fatalistic love after the first brief ecstasy. Symons emphasises the frustrations and bitterness of the lovers' situation, showing Tristram as overwhelmed by these and devoured by Iseult's flame instead of by a mutual kindling. Iseult implies as much as she mourns his death:

> This dust was a fire and burned the stars:
> Now what little ashes holds the fire
> That was blown out too early. There is nothing
> Left in the world, and I am out of place.

Thomas Hardy's play, *The Famous Tragedy of the Queen of Cornwall* (1923), presents us with a very different and more active version of Tristram's death. The structure of the play is unusual, and harks back to Greek tragedy with its use of male and female choruses to comment on the action. Hardy combines the tradition of Malory with that of the early writers, using the latter as background but the former for the action of the play itself. Mark it is who kills Tristram; Hardy adds his own sequel, Iseult's killing of Mark and suicide.

Hardy declared that he had 'tried to avoid turning the rude personages of, say, the fifth century into respectable Victorians, as was done by Tennyson, Swinburne, Arnold etc.' He chose an archaic vocabulary, and believed that by underplaying the dramatic side of the acting the play could achieve a 'curiously hypnotising' effect. On the page, it offers nothing more than a certain strangeness: a conscious attempt at a medieval play every bit as anachronistic as the Victorian works he so decried. The characters have a rough-hewn quality but belong to Hardy's Wessex rather than a Court in whatever age. It is a minor, curious work from a master's hand, with rare flashes of greater illumination.

Yet another version of the Tristram legend comes from the pen of an American writer. E.A. Robinson's poem *Tristram* (1928), awarded the Pulitzer Prize for that year, is more in the tradition of Arnold than Swinburne; the love potion is entirely absent, and the lovers die by Andret's hand. Robinson observes not the ecstasy of passionate love, but the resulting torment:

> And for a time nothing was to be heard
> Except the pounding of two hearts in prison,
> The torture of a doom-begotten music
> Above them, and the wash of a cold foam
> Below them on those cold eternal rocks
> Where Tristram and Iseult had yesterday
> Come to be wrecked together. When her eyes
> Opened again, he saw there, watching him,
> An aching light of memory; and his heart beat,
> Beat harder for remembering the same light
> That he had seen before in the same eyes.

Here is no serene security in requited love, but an anguished, doubting passion full of deeps and shadows. Yet it is the portrait of Iseult of

15 Miniatures from Wolfram von Eschenbach's *Parzival*. Top: Parzival at Arthur's court. Centre: Parzival and another count in single combat. Bottom: Parzival and his half-brother Feirefiz. From a German manuscript of *c.* 1250

16 Miniature from Wolfram von Eschenbach's *Parzival*. Top: Parzival and Feirefiz at Arthur's camp. Centre: Kundrig arrives at Arthur's court summoning Parzival to the Grail Castle. Bottom: Parzival, Feirefiz and Kundrig arrive at the Grail Castle. From a German manuscript of *c.* 1250

17 Left: Perceval arrives at the Grail Castle.
Right: the Grail is carried in procession,
together with the Holy Lance. From a
manuscript of Chrétien de Troyes' *Conte del Graal*

18 A miniature illustrating
Chrétien de Troyes' poem
Yvain. Left: Lunete in prison.
Right: Yvain fights a giant.
Below: Yvain rescues Lunete
with the help of his tame
lion

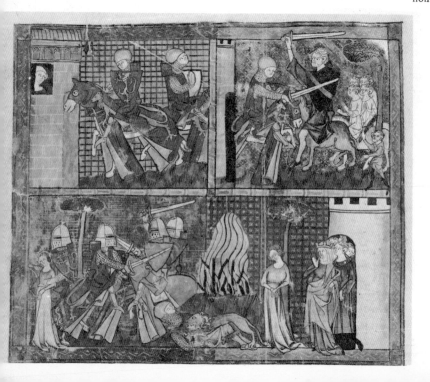

19 Sicilian quilt, *c.* 1295, with scenes from the story of Tristan

20 Lancelot crossing the Sword Bridge. Thirteenth-century capital from St Pierre, Caen

21 and 22 Thirteenth-century tiles from Chertsey Abbey. Above: Tristan plays the harp for King Mark. Below: Tristan and Iseult sail to Cornwall

Galahad is given
key to the Castle
Maidens, where he
frees the captives
the enchantment
that keeps them
prisoners there.
Ivory, *c.* 1320

24   Far left: Gawain fights
a lion. Left: Lancelot on
the Sword Bridge. Right:
Gawain on the Perilous
Bed. Far right: three ladies.
Ivory casket, Parisian,
c. 1325

25 King Arthur as one of the Nine Worthies. Statue of *c.* 1480, from the Hofkirche at Innsbruck by Peter Visscher

26 **Queen** Guinevere, drawing by William Morris, 1858

27 The popular ideal of King
Arthur: engraving from a
Victorian periodical, *c.* 1860–70

28 *Mort d'Arthur* by Frederic G.
Stephens, *c.* 1850–5

29   *Arthur's Tomb:* 'How Sir Lancelot
parted from Queen Guinevere at King
Arthur's tomb, and would have kissed her
at parting, but she would not', by
Dante Gabriel Rossetti, 1855

30   'A modern vision of Guinevere, by the
artist and poet, David Jones, 1940–1.
David Jones' long poems *In Parenthesis*
and *The Anathemata* contain references
to the legends of Arthur.

Brittany – as in Arnold – that emerges most vividly; her quiet watching for him, even after she has learnt of his death, closes the poem:

> ... Isolt of the white hands,
> Isolt with her grey eyes and her white face,
> Still gazed across the water for the north.
> But not now for a ship ...
>   ... Yet there she gazed
> Across the water, over the white waves,
> Upon a castle that she had never seen,
> And would not see, save as a phantom shape
> Against a phantom sky. He had been there,
> She thought, but not with her. He had died there,
> But not for her. He had not thought of her,
> Perhaps, and that was strange. He had been all,
> And would be always all there was for her,
> And he had not come back to her alive,
> Not even to go again.

This clear-sighted and tender poem is the best American contribution to the legend yet.

John Masefield's *Midsummer Night and other tales in verse* (1927) presents us with a series of linked pictures and incidents that cover the main events of the life of Arthur. He draws on a wide range of sources, both classical and medieval, sometimes going back to early Welsh material, sometimes offering his own alternative versions of the legend. *The Begetting of Arthur*, at the opening of the cycle, has two such versions: one is a tragic love-story, in which Uther is slain by Ygerne's father, Merchyon, after one brief night of love as a result of which Arthur is born. The other, *The Old Tale of the Begetting*, begins:

> The men of old that made the tale for us
> Declare that Uther begot Arthur thus

and continues with the story told by Geoffrey of Monmouth. The next two poems, on the birth of Mordred, rely on Malory, except that Morgause becomes Arthur's aunt instead of his half-sister. Arthur's hour of triumph is represented by *Badon Hill*, in which he slaughters his Saxon enemies; and his connection with the mysteries of the other world is portrayed in *The Sailing of Hell Race*, a new version of *The Spoils of Annwfn*[1] in which Arthur visits the three kingdoms of hell, each with its allegorical rulers – Self and Mammon, War, Sloth and Pestilence.

The legends which follow set the tragedy in motion, which is brought about by Arthur's love for Guinevere and its consequences. In *Arthur and his Ring*, Masefield borrows the classical story of the lover who slips his beloved's ring onto the finger of a statue of Venus, and has to beg it of the goddess herself before he can regain it. *Midsummer Night*, echoing the tale of Arthur's survival in a cave in a sleep from which he awakens each Midsummer night, allows each of the characters involved to explain their part in the remorseless working of fate. The remaining poems tell the familiar story, save for the appearance of Mordred's wife Gwenivach as a protagonist of her husband's treachery. And by way of epilogue Masefield portrays Henry II at the grave of Arthur, setting against this vision of mortality and history another poem, *On The Coming of Arthur*, in praise of his immortal spirit.

Masefield's work is in an unfashionable medium, a series of historical ballads, in ballad metre; and it is difficult to estimate their true worth. His handling of plot and character is strong, but the ballad form itself has a comfortable homeliness about it that ill consorts with the high romanticism of the story. For this is still an idealised treatment, for all its would-be realism. Masefield has a vivid way of lighting up a figure: Mordred's outburst of hatred – 'Thirty years' anguish made by your idle lust' – strikes home, as does Arthur's helpless and equivocal relationship with his son and Guinevere looking at Lancelot in death: 'I had not thought of him as old.' And the cycle is well balanced, moving forward with the ease of the true story-teller, save for the digression of *Arthur and his Ring*. Yet in the end it is not the great version of the legend that it promises at moments to become, because Masefield has not really come to terms with his theme, and the novelty of his use of different material to tell the same story, the dependence on Welsh sources or recent research, is no substitute for the inner spiritual power that the subject demands. The moral element is slight and uncertainly conventional, the poetic effect limited by the form chosen. It is a fine retelling, but not a renewal, of various Arthurian aspects skilfully woven into new formations.

This renewal is achieved by a very different poet from Masefield, Charles Williams, in his two volumes *Taliessin through Logres* and *The Region of the Summer Stars*. In essence, though not in detail, it is an extension of Tennyson's vision of Arthur as ideal man, for in Williams' poems Arthur's kingdom of Lorges is to be the perfect union between earth and heaven. The symbolism is involved to the point of being at moments laboured, and C. S. Lewis' exposition of it in *Arthurian Torso* is invaluable as an approach and guide. The poems are dominated by the concept of the Roman and Byzantine Empires seen most clearly in *The Vision of the Empire*. The image is that of a reclining female figure. The 'skull-stone' is the rocky outer edge of Britain/Lorgres, which stands as the Empire's soul and brain. The breasts are in Gaul, where the schools of Paris, famous in the Middle Ages, provide the nourishing milk of learning. On Rome the hands lie clasped: here the Pope says Mass with its 'heart-breaking manual acts'. Jerusalem is the womb, from which Adam, fallen man, came. Caucasia is the 'fool's shame', the bottom of the figure. Lastly there is Byzantium, the navel, in which all the 'dialects' arise and re-echo. These are the 'themes' of the Empire, which are related in the same way as the body.

There is an antithesis to the Empire, on the other side of the world, in P'o-Lu, where the headless Emperor of the Antipodes walks. This is the consequence of the Fall: bodies become shameful instead of a glory of creation, and so here the 'feet of creation' walk backwards. For in P'o-Lu are the feet of the Empire, and they are feet of clay. It is from here that the failure of Arthur's mission springs.

At the opposite extreme, beyond Logres, lies the Wood of Broceliande – a sea-wood, Williams calls it – and beyond a certain part of it, Carbonek, the castle in which the Grail is kept. Beyond this and a stretch of open sea, is Sarras, the home of the Grail. It is towards this that Arthur's mission and the whole feeling of the poems tend, reflecting Williams' deep religious and mystical attitudes.

163

Through Broceliande lies the way from earth to heaven – as witness the Grail city and castle. But Williams insists that these last lie beyond only a certain part of it. If one goes far enough the Antipodes may be reached through these same regions. C. S. Lewis explains this apparent contradiction as follows:

> In a writer whose philosophy was Pantheistic or whose poetry was merely romantic, this formidable wood ... would undoubtedly figure as the Absolute itself ... All journeys away from the solid earth are equally, at the outset journeys into the abyss. Saint, sorcerer, lunatic and romantic lover, all alike are drawn to Broceliande, but Carbonek is beyond a certain part of it only. It is by no means the Absolute. It is rather what the Greeks called the Apeiron – the unlimited, the formless origin of forms.

Such then is the geography, physical and spiritual, of Williams' world. Against this background Arthur, Taliessin and Merlin work out their mission. Nimue, lady of Broceliande, sends her children, Merlin and Brisen, to perform the great task of perfect union. They meet Taliessin, still the pagan poet of Wales, as they go to create the kingdom of balanced humanity, an earthly kingdom parallel to the holy kingdom of Carbonek, in which the Empire and Broceliande, the physical, the intellectual and the spiritual shall meet. Arthur is to be their instrument; they depart for Logres, and Taliessin for Byzantium.

Taliessin's part in the mission is not immediately clear, but we learn that on his return from Byzantium he bears with him the vision of the Empire, standing for order, which he must impose on the as yet chaotic Logres; this must be accomplished before the Grail can come to dwell there. He is also the type of the poet, which is bound up in his personal task. The poet, in Williams' view, cannot inspire love for himself, yet can inspire others to it; this is illustrated in *Taliessin's song of the Unicorn*, where the poet is likened to the legendary unicorn, attracted to a virgin; she will not love him, and her lover will come and kill the creature out of jealousy.

Taliessin's mission is a success, and the Golden Age of Logres ensues. The lyric pieces which describe this involve various philosophical concepts, but centre on the nature of love. The last of these is *The Coming of Palomides*; Palomides, learned in Arabic science, looks on Iseult and admires the geometrical beauty of her form. But as he dreams of the first kind of love, physical consummation, the Questing Beast

> . . . scratched itself in the blank between
> The Queen's substance and the Queen.

He must find the answer to the connection between the flesh and the spirit before he can find intellectual love.

But the plan as a whole is doomed to failure: the actual deeds which prevent Logres from becoming the kingdom of the Grail are Arthur's unwitting incest with Morgause, and Balin's equally unconscious slaying of his brother and giving of the Dolorous Blow. Both pairs act blindly; it is not their individual fault that these things are done, but the fault of human nature, of fallen man, operating deep below the surface of Logres.

Yet out of this failure springs a measure of success. The Grail cannot come to Logres; but the uncorrupted part of Logres may reach the Grail. It is again Taliessin's task to prepare the way. The company of his household are his instrument; at the base of their efforts lies salvation worked through poetry and the senses, Taliessin's own special task. It is Taliessin as head of this 'Company of the Redeemed' who greets the first of the future Grail band to arrive at Court, Percivale and his sister Blanchefleur. By the machinations of Merlin and Brisen, Galahad is born, at the cost of the sanity of his father Lancelot, for which Galahad later atones. He is delivered into Blanchefleur's care, and the space of his youth is filled by one poem only: *Palomides before his Christening*. Palomides has failed in his quest; intellectual love is not for him. But through disillusionment comes his conversion to Christianity, if only as a belief in disbelief.

The coming of Galahad takes place on the evening of Palomides' christening, and we hear of it from Taliessin, Gareth and a slave as they discuss it afterwards. One of the more important images here is drawn from Book Five of Wordsworth's *The Prelude*. The stone and shell borne by the Arab in this poem are fitted in Galahad; the union which was to have been Logres has been fulfilled in one man only.

None save three will succeed, and reach Carbonek; the rest will sink into Britain. The forces of Broceliande depart. Palomides finds the answer to his problem; what he had seen as ends in themselves, love, fame, irony, were only paths to a greater end, and, happy in this knowledge, he dies.

The climax and simultaneously the anti-climax are now reached. The Grail is achieved at the expense of the Round Table. So triumph on the one hand, in *Percivale at Carbonek* and *The Last Voyage* are balanced by the implied disaster of *The Meditation of Mordred* and *The Prayers of the Pope*. As the Grail is achieved, and withdrawn to Sarras, Logres sinks into the chaos out of which it had risen. Taliessin dissolves his company, but they gather for the last time, in flesh or in spirit, at the Mass performed by Lancelot. The mission has reached its end; all that could or can ever be achieved has been achieved. Lancelot's voice singing '*Ite; missa est*' is the signal for the irrevocable dispersal, and 'that which was once Taliessin' rides slowly away.

The poems are symbolic and sometimes obscure in concept; the poet in Williams struggles, sometimes unsuccessfully, with the philosopher. But the verse itself is brilliant in its incantation, and the words flow in a strange music. Here are two contrasting examples. Taliessin comes to Lancelot's Mass at the end of the cycle:

I came to his altar when dew was bright on the grass:
He – he was not sworn of the priesthood – began the Mass.
The altar was an ancient stone laid upon stones;
Carbonek's arch, Camelot's wall, frame of Bors' bones.

In armour before the earthen footpace he stood;
On his surcoat the lions of his house, dappled with blood,
Rampant, regardant; but he wore no helm or sword,
And his hands were bare as Lateran's to the work of our Lord.

But this is less typical than the following passage, the climax of Merlin's and Brisen's incantations at the launching of the mission:

The stars vanished; they gone, the illumined dusk
Under the spell darkened to the colour of porphyry,

166

The colour of the stair of Empire and the womb of women,
And the rich largesse of the Emperor; within was a point,
Deep beyond or deep within Logres,
As if it had swallowed all the summer stars.
And hollowed the porphyry night for its having and hiding –
Tiny, dark-rose, self-glowing,
As a firefly's egg or (beyond body and spirit,
Could the art of the king's poet in the court of Camelot,
After his journeys, find words for body or spirit)
The entire point of the thrice co-inherent Trinity
When every crown and every choir is vanished,
And all sight and hearing is nothing else.

Williams has used the Arthurian legend as the mould for his indiv-idual and intensely Christian philosophy. While the matter and events of the old tales are retained, characters and values are totally different. Yet this, in its mystical way, is one of the great works of Arthurian literature. It is a heightening of Tennyson's moral vision into mysticism, the spiritual application of Swinburne's intense study of physical love within the framework of the legend.

T. H. White's *The Once and Future King* is also a very individual work, but of a totally different kind. It is a modern retelling of Malory in which 'all the characters are the same, save that Pellinore has a love-affair, and the fact that Lancelot is ugly'. But there is one further very important difference: White has tempered the story with com-edy, which for the first time in the Arthurian stories is successful comedy, even if very much of the moment, and centres chiefly on Merlin as an absent-minded magician. The exposition of Malory is often worth a dozen essays on the subject, and White takes his story as an 'Aristotelian tragedy', in which the crux is the political and spiritual question so well put by Charles Williams:

The king made for the kingdom, or the kingdom made for the king?

In Williams, Arthur offers the wrong solution, and this is partly why he fails. Here Merlin directs Arthur's education with the sole aim of making him a king for the kingdom. Only Mordred, born of human weakness, can bring about his downfall by exploiting the love of Lancelot and Guinevere.

167

White succeeds best in two aspects of the story. His characters are convincing, and Arthur emerges a real human being rather than a symbol; where Malory glosses over his feelings, White uses the techniques of the modern novelist to draw them for us, as when, despite his insistence on doing his duty as King, he nonetheless hopes that Lancelot will rescue Guinevere from the stake. Gawain and his brothers are strongly depicted: the sullen Agravaine, gentle loyal Gareth and Gaheris, and Mordred, their bitter, tortured half-brother. Only Lancelot and Guinevere lose a little of their aura in the re-telling.

The evocation of England in the Middle Ages is masterly, and here White's delightful and wide funds of knowledge come into their own, whether it be on his own favourite subject of hawking, practice for a tournament, a siege, or merely the details of everyday life in a medieval castle, all of which he conveys deftly and entertainingly, without letting the reader suspect that he is being given an expert lesson.

With this, our survey of King Arthur and his place in history and literature draws to a close. One large question remains: what is the secret of Arthur's continuing popularity as a heroic figure, and why – if indeed a reason can be given – should he reappear so dramatically in the twelfth and nineteenth centuries? It is understandable that the Welsh should focus their hopes on a national Messiah, but it is more difficult to see his attraction for medieval France or Victorian England.

The rapid spread of Arthurian romance in the twelfth century was due to a larger literary movement. In those years, the literatures and languages of modern Europe were just beginning to emerge. Latin, the normal language of anything other than everyday matters, was beginning to retreat into the schools and churches in face of the rising spirit of nationalism throughout the Continent. The Norse and Celtic countries alone possessed a vernacular literature of any size and interest, and contact between the two cultures was rare until the

Normans invaded England. The English vernacular was admittedly a language of some standing, but it was temporarily overwhelmed, and had less influence than the cultures of the still independent peoples on the borders of the newly-conquered land. The Celtic races possessed what the Latin peoples lacked to a large extent, a popular epic repertoire with immediate appeal. It was only natural that these tales, as they were gradually diffused, should be eagerly taken up as poetic subjects by the writers of the new vernacular.

The nineteenth-century revival was more a literary movement from the outset, with its roots in the growing scholarship of the eighteenth century on medieval matters, which in turn stemmed from a reaction against the domination of classical ideals. But it was only where a poet found them relevant to the problems which interested him, as Tennyson did in England and Wagner in Germany, that the revival was more than mere antiquarianism. English writers, with Malory's easily accessible complete version of Arthur's career available, were at an advantage; and it was easy for them to present Arthur as a national hero once more, as part of a proud heritage now being triumphantly fulfilled in the Victorian Age.

Why then does King Arthur still live in the imagination of modern man, in a far different, crueller world? Perhaps because he is an historical enigma, an intriguing question-mark in the past; perhaps because the romances give us an unrivalled insight into the medieval mind; perhaps because the stories contain human situations paralleled in our age; perhaps because they remind us of a lost idealism. But there is one transcending and much simpler reason why the Arthurian legends will continue to be read, which Caxton gave five centuries ago: because in them we shall find 'many joyous and plysaunt hystoryes and noble and renomed acts of humanyte, gentylenesse and chyvalryes'. As long as poetry is written, Arthur will be remembered; he may yet have many vicissitudes to come, but the legends are so integral a part of our heritage that his figure will always emerge again, mysterious, heroic, and yet human.

Notes

Chapter 3: Arthur the Emperor

1 This practice of inventing founders of countries, by using a supposed
character in classical legend with a similar name, was common in medieval
writers. Four examples are given in the first stanza of *Sir Gawain and the
Green Knight:* Romulus for Rome, Ticius for Tuscany, Longbeard for Lombardy
and Brutus for Britain.

2 See chapter 7.

3 In Geoffrey of Monmouth's account he does not even cross the Alps into
Italy.

Chapter 4: Arthur and Avalon

1 On this important point there is unfortunately wide variance as to translation.
Another version reads: 'An eternal wonder is the grave of Arthur.' But the
underlying implication is agreed to be that Arthur's death was mysterious,
and the possibility of this return was hinted at.

2 MS Arthurus.

3 MS Wenneveria.

4 MS Avallonia.

5 The description of Guinevere as his second wife may come from the legend
of the true and false Guineveres, which is of Welsh origin, and was current
at the time (*cf.* Vulgate Merlin, *c.* 1230).

6 For examples of the difficulties in dealing with Tudor drawings of archaeological material, see T. Kendrick, *British Antiquity* (London 1953), pp. 162–3,
where three variant versions of the so-called Doniert stone in Cornwall are
illustrated.

7 There is also a non-Arthurian version from Swaffham in Norfolk.

Chapter 5: The Matter of Britain: Romances in French

1 There were two other great cycles of stories the Charlemagne romances, or *matière de France*, and the stories about Alexander, or *matière de Grèce*.

Chapter 6: Tristan and Parzival: the German Romances

1 i.e. Galehault, Lancelot and Guinevere's go-between.

Chapter 7: The English Poems

1 'Let him who wishes to, set out in verse the fine points of a battle-axe: the head was a full yard in length, the sides of green steel decorated with gold; the edge was burnished and broad, as well shaped for cutting as sharp razors. The shaft was a strong staff, its handle bound with iron to the foot, and skilfully engraved in green.'

2 'Now the New Year draws near, and the night passes; daylight drives off darkness, as our Lord ordained. But the world outside was full of wild weather; the clouds cast bitter cold on the earth that came from the north and caused the flesh pain; the snow fell bleakly, and froze the wild beasts; the whirling wind wailed from the heights, and filled each valley with great drifts. The knight [ie. Gawain] listened as he lay in bed; though his eyes were closed, he slept but little, and knew the hour by the cock's crowing.'

3 'When he rode through the countryside, his armour glistened like gold, as he rode on his way. He saw many wonders there; birds fled across the water, by lakes and banks so broad. He saw many wonders there, of wolves and wild beasts, and paid much attention to hunting; in truth, he rode out to seek the Green Chapel, and he had not idea where it was.'

4 'He scaled many a cliff in strange country, riding far from his friends, forsaken. At every ford or stream that he passed he found a foe before him, save by some strange chance; and they were so foul and strange that he had to fight them. So many marvels did he meet in the mountains that it would be wearisome to tell you the tenth of them. Sometimes he fought with dragons and wolves as well, sometimes with wild men that dwelt in the crags; and he fought both with bulls, bears and boars, as well as giants that attacked him on the moors: if he had not been doughty and strong and served the Lord, he would certainly have died and often been defeated. For warfare did not weary him so much as the winter, which was far worse, when the cold clear water was shed from the clouds, freezing before it could fall

to the fallow earth: almost dead from the sleet he slept in his armour, night after night, among the bare rocks, where cold streams rang clattering down from the peaks and hung high over his head in hard icicles. Thus in peril and pain and many a hard plight, this knight crossed the countryside until Christmas Eve all alone. And then the knight made his prayer to the Virgin, that She would guide him until he came to some dwelling.'

5 'With a keen sword, sturdy and sharp, which had often been his companion and stay in battle, he attacked the man, furious with pain, and cut through the corner of the bright shield, through his mail and breast-plate and border; the ornament of fine gold fell to the ground. Red blood gushed out along the blade in spite of all the armour he was wearing; it went through gold clasps and bright fastening. At this Sir Golagros in great wrath, fierce as fire, let fly at his foe.'

Chapter 9: An Enduring Fame

1 See chapter 2 above.

Chronological List of Arthurian Literature

Key: (pr) prose work; (p) poem; (d) drama; (tr) tragedy; (n) novel;
    (ed) edition; (trs) translation; (Fr) French; (Ger) German;
    (D) Dutch; (I) Italian; (L) Latin; (W) Welsh.

c. 550   Gildas, *De Excidio Britanniae* (L)
c. 600   *The Gododdin* (W p)
c. 700   Adomnan, *Life of Columba* (L)
c. 800–20   Nennius, *Historia Britonum* (L)
c. 960   *Annales Cambriae* (L)
c. 1080–1100   *Culhwch and Olwen* (W pr)
c. 1110–20   Modena sculpture
1135   Geoffrey of Monmouth, *Prophetia Merlini* (L pr)
1136   Geoffrey of Monmouth, *Historia Regum Britanniae* (L pr)
c. 1150   First version of *Tristan* (Fr p)
1151   Geoffrey of Monmouth, *Vita Merlini* (L p)
1155   Wace, *Roman de Brut* (Fr p)
c. 1160–80   Marie de France, *Lais* (Fr p)
          Thomas, *Tristan* (Fr p)
c. 1170   Chrétien de Troyes, *Erec* (Fr p)
          Eilhart von Oberge, *Tristan* (Ger p)
c. 1176   Chrétien de Troyes, *Cligès* (Fr p)
c. 1180   Chrétien de Troyes, *Lancelot* and *Yvain* (Fr p)
c. 1185–90   Renart de Beaujeu, *Le Bel Inconnu* (Fr p)
c. 1190   Layamon, *Brut* (p)
          Béroul, *Tristan* (Fr p)
          Chrétien de Troyes, *Perceval* (Fr p)
          Hartmann von Aue, *Erek* (Ger p)
c. 1190–1210   *Perlesvaus* (Fr pr)

c. **1200** First and second continuations of *Perceval* (Fr p)
Ulrich von Zatzikhoven, *Lanzelet* (Ger p)
Jaufré (Fr p)
Gereint, Owein, Peredur (W pr)

c. 1200–10 Wolfram von Eschenbach, *Parzival* (Ger p)
Robert de Boron, *Joseph d'Arimathie* and *Merlin* (Fr p)

c. 1202 Hartmann von Aue, *Iwein* (Ger p)

c. 1210 Gottfried von Strassburg, *Tristan* (Ger p)
Wirnt von Gravenberg, *Wigalois* (Ger p)
Le Chevalier à l'Epée (Fr p)

c. 1210–20 Manessier, continuation of *Perceval* (Fr p)
? *Didot Perceval* (Fr pr)
La Mule sans Fresne (Fr p)
La Vengeance Raguidel (Fr p)

c. 1210–25 *Yder* (Fr p)

c. 1215–30 *Vulgate Cycle* (Fr pr)

c. 1220 Heinrich von dem Türlin, *Diû Krone* (Ger p)

c. 1220–50 *Durmart le Gallois* (Fr. p)
Gliglois (Fr p)

c. 1225 Raoul de Houdenc, *Meraugis de Portlesguez* (Fr p)
Fergus (Fr p)

c. 1225–35 *Prose Tristan* (Fr)
Meriaduc (Fr p)

1226 Brother Robert, *Tristramssaga* (Norse p)

c. 1230–40 *Suite du Merlin* and *Roman du Graal* (Fr pr)
Erex saga and *Ivens saga* (Norse p)

c. 1235–40 *Palamedes* (Fr pr)

c. 1250 *L'atre perilleux* (Fr p)
Walewein (D p)

c. 1250–75 *Prose Tristan* (second version) (Fr)

c. 1250–1300 *Arthour and Merlin* (p)
Humbaut (Fr p)
Floriant et Florete (Fr p)

c. 1268 *Claris et Laris* (Fr p)

c. 1260–90 *Les Merveilles de Rigomer* (Fr p)

1261–1326 Dutch *Joseph* and *Merlin* cycle (p)

c. 1272–9 *Les Propheties de Merlin* (Fr pr)

c. 1280 *Escanor* (Fr p)
Meriadocus (L pr)
De ortu Walwanii (L pr)

1300 onwards Spanish and Portuguese translations of the Vulgate Cycle
and other major romances; various versions of the *Tristan*
in Italian

c. 1300   *Arthur and Gorlagon* (L pr)
           Sir Tristrem (p)
1303   *Herra Ivan* (Norse p)
c. 1300–20   Dutch *Lancelot* cycle (p)
c. 1320–40   *Libeaus Desconus* (p)
           Sir Percyvelle of Galles (p)
           Sir Launfal (p)
c. 1350   *Ywain and Gawain* (p)
c. 1350–1400   *Arthur* (p)
c. 1360   Alliterative *Morte Arthure* (p)
c. 1375–1400   Tuscan *cantari* on Arthurian themes
           Awntyrs of Arthure (p)
c. 1390   *Gawain and the Green Knight* (p)
           Froissart, *Meliador* (Fr p)
c. **1400**   *Le Chevalier du Papegau* (**Fr** pr)
           Stanzaic *Morte Arthur* (p)
           The Carl of Carlisle (p)
c. 1425   *The Avowing of King Arthur* (p)
c. 1430   Lovelich's *Holy Grail* and *Merlin* (p)
c. 1450   *The Gest of Sir Gawain* (p)
           The Wedding of Sir Gawain (p)
1470   Sir Thomas Malory, *Morte Darthur* (pr)
c. 1480–90   *Lancelot du Laik* (p)
           Golagros and Gawain (p)
1485   Caxton's edition of Malory
1500–50   English ballads
           French and Spanish printed romances
1510   *Little Tretys of the Birth and Prophecies of Merlin* (pr)
1553   Hans Sachs, *Von der strenge lieb herr Tristrant mit der schönen königin*
           Isalden (Ger tr)
1570   Luigi Alamanni, *L'Avarchide* (Italian p)
1587   Thomas Hughes, *The Misfortunes of Arthur* (tr)
1590–6   Edmund Spenser, *The Faerie Queene* (p)
1610   Richard Johnson, *Romance of Tom a Lincolne* (pr)
1640   Martin Parker, *History of Arthur* (pr)
1691   John Dryden, *King Arthur* (opera; music by Purcell)
1695   Sir Richard Blackmore, *Prince Arthur* (p)
1697   Sir Richard Blackmore, *King Arthur* (p)
1730   Henry Fielding, *The Tragedy of Tragedies* (d)
1771   Christoph Wieland, *Sommermärchen* (Ger p)
1775–80   Comte de la Vergue de Tressan, *Extraits de romans de chevalerie* in
           Bibliothèque universelle des romans (Fr p)
1777   Thomas Warton, *Grave of King Arthur* (p)

1778	Christoph Wieland, *Geron der Adelige* (Ger p)
1804	Sir Walter Scott, ed. and completed *Sir Tristrem*
1812	Baron Creuzé de Lesser, *Les Chevaliers de la Table Ronde* (Fr p)
1813	Sir Walter Scott, *The Bridal of Triermain* (p)
1826	Robert Southey's edition of Malory
1829	Thomas Love Peacock, *Misfortunes of Elphin*
1830	William Wordsworth, *The Egyptian Maid* (p)
1832	Alfred Lord Tennyson, *The Lady of Shalott* (p)
	Karl Immermann, *Merlin* (Ger pr)
1838	Lady Charlotte Guest, *The Mabinogion* (trs fr W)
1841	Reginald Heber, *Morte Arthure* (p)
1842	Alfred Lord Tennyson, *Sir Launcelot and Queen Guinevere, Sir Galahad Morte d'Arthur* (p)
1848	Lord Lytton, *King Arthur* (p)
1852	Matthew Arnold, *Tristram and Iseult* (p)
1856	F. Roeber, *Tristran und Isolde* (Ger p)
1858	William Morris, *The Defence of Guinevere* and other poems
1859	Alfred Lord Tennyson, *Idylls of the King I* (p)
	Edgar Quinet, *Merlin l'Enchanteur* (Fr pr)
	Richard Wagner, *Tristan und Isolde* (opera)
1860	Wilhelm Hertz, *Lanzelot und Genevra* (Ger p)
1863	R. S. Hawker, *Quest of the Sangreal* (p)
1865	L. Schneegans, *Tristan* (Ger p)
1868	Adam Lindsay Gordon, *Rhyme of Joyous Garde* (p)
1869	G. A. Simcox, *Farewell of Ganore* (p), *Gawain and the Lady of Avalon* (p)
	Alfred Lord Tennyson, *Idylls II* (p)
1870	F. Millard, *Tristram and Iseult* (p)
1880	J. R. Lowell, *Sir Launfal* (p)
1882	Richard Wagner, *Parsifal* (opera)
	Algernon Swinburne, *Tristram of Lyonesse* (p)
1885	Alfred Lord Tennyson, *Idylls III* (p)
1889	Alfred Lord Tennyson, *Merlin and the Gleam* (p)
	John Veitch, *Merlin and other poems* (p)
1891	R. Hovey, *Lancelot and Guinevere* (d)
1895	J. Comyns Carr, *King Arthur* (d)
1896	Algernon Swinburne, *Tale of Balen* (p)
1898	J. Davidson, *The Last Ballad* (p)
1900	J. Bédier, *Le Roman de Tristran et Iseult* (Fr pr)
1911	Michael Field, *Tragedy of Pardon, Tristan de Leonois* (tr)
1913	Laurence Binyon, *Tristram's End* (p)
1917	Arthur Symons, *Tristram and Iseult* (tr)
1923	Thomas Hardy, *The Queen of Cornwall* (tr)
1927	John Masefield, *Midsummer Night* (p), *Tristan and Isolt* (tr)

1928   E. A. Robinson, *Tristan* (p)
1938   Charles Williams, *Taliessin through Logres* (p)
1942   Frank Martin, *Le Vin Herbe* (oratorio; text Bédier)
1944   Charles Williams, *The Region of the Summer Stars* (p)
1958   T. H. White, *The Once and Future King* (n)

Select Bibliography

The following list concentrates on texts and translations, and on major critical works. Textual editions are not given for works after 1500, nor for Continental works.

Chapter 1

GILDAS: *De Excidio Britanniae* tr. and ed. Hugh Williams, Cymmrodrion Soc., London, 1899.

NENNIUS: *Historia Brittonum* ed. Ferdinand Lot, *Nennius et l'Historia Brittonum*, Paris, 1934; tr. A. W. Wade-Evans, *Nennius' 'History of the Britons'* etc., London, 1938.

ANNALES CAMBRIAE: ed. Egerton Phillimore, 'The *Annales Cambriae* and the Old-Welsh Genealogies from Harleian MS 3859', *Y Cymmrodor* 9, 1888, 141–83.

THE GODODDIN: tr. Kenneth Jackson, *The Gododdin*, Edinburgh, 1969.

K. H. Jackson, 'The Arthur of History', in *Arthurian Literature in the Middle Ages* ed. R. S. Loomis, Oxford, 1959, 1–11.

Robert W. Hanning, *The Vision of History in Early Britain*, New York and London, 1966.

Leslie Alcock, *Arthur's Britain*, London and New York, 1971 (chiefly archaeology).

Richard Barber, *The Figure of Arthur*, London, 1972 (Argues for Arthur of Dalriada; full bibliography).

John Morris, *The Age of Arthur*, London, 1973 (An attempt, not very convincingly, to restore the traditional view of Romano British Arthur).

Chapter 2

Rachel Bromwich, (ed. and trs.) *Trioedd Ynys Prydein: The Welsh Triads*, Cardiff, 1961.

Thomas Jones, 'The early evolution of the legend of Arthur', *Nottingham Medieval Studies* VIII, 1964 3–21.

E. K. Chambers, *Arthur of Britain*, London, 1927, reissued Cambridge, 1964 (Includes translations)

R. S. Loomis, *Wales and the Arthurian Legend*, Cardiff, 1956.

Chapter 3

GEOFFREY OF MONMOUTH: *Historia Regum Britanniae*, ed. A. Griscom, London and New York, 1929; tr. Lewis Thorpe, *The History of the Kings of Britain*, Harmondsworth, 1966.

WACE AND LAYAMON: tr. L. A. Paton, *Arthurian Chronicles represented by Wace and Layamon*, London, 1912, reprinted 1970.

MORTE ARTHURE: ed. M. M. Banks, EETS, London, 1900; reissued 1970.

R. A. Fletcher, *The Arthurian Material in the Chronicles*, Cambridge, Mass., 1906.

J. P. S. Tatlock, *The Legendary History of Britain*, Los Angeles, 1950.

Chapter 4

J. Armitage Robinson, *Two Glastonbury Legends*, Cambridge, 1926.

R. F. Treharne, *The Glastonbury Legends: Joseph of Arimathea, The Holy Grail and King Arthur*, London, 1967.

Chapter 5

R. S. Loomis (ed.) *Arthurian Literature in the Middle Ages*, Oxford, 1959.

CHRÉTIEN DE TROYES: *Erec, Cligés, Lancelot, Yvain*, tr. W. W. Comfort, *Arthurian Romances by Chrétien de Troyes*, London, 1914.

Jean Frappier, *Chrétien de Troyes*, Paris, 1968.

THOMAS: ed. & tr. R. S. Loomis, *The Romance of Tristram and Ysolt*, New York, 1951.

BÉROUL: ed. J. Bédier, tr. H. Belloc, *The Romance of Tristan and Iseult*, London, 1936.

DIDOT PERCEVAL: tr. Dell Skeels, *The Romance of Perceval in Prose*, Seattle, 1961.

QUESTE DEL SAINT GRAAL: tr. Pauline Matrasso, *The Quest of the Holy Grail*, Harmondsworth, 1969.

LA MORT ARTU: tr. James Cable, *The Death of King Arthur*, Harmondsworth, 1971.

PERLESVAUS: tr. Sebastian Evans, *The High History of the Holy Grail*, London, 1912 (Introduction on date and author inaccurate).

R. S. Loomis, *Arthurian Tradition and Chrétien de Troyes*, New York, 1949.

Chapter 6

WOLFRAM VON ESCHENBACH: *Parzival*, tr. Edwin Zeydel and Bayard Q. Morgan, Chapel Hill, 1951.

GOTTFRIED VON STRASSBURG: *Tristan*, tr. (with *Tristan* of Thomas) A. T. Hatto, Harmondsworth, 1960.

Hugh Sacker, *An Introduction to Wolfram's Parzival*, Cambridge, 1963.

Chapter 7

There are editions of *Gawain and the Green Knight* (1940), *Ywain and Gawain* (1964), *Lybeaus Desconus* (1969), *Le Morte Arthur* (1891) and *Lancelot of the Laik* (rptd 1965) in the Early English Text Society series. Modern versions by J. L. Weston include: *Romances unrepresented in Malory*, London, 1902 (Libeaus Desconus), *Chief Middle English Poets*, Boston, 1914 (*Sir Percyvelle of Galles* and *Sir Tristrem*). There are several modern versions of *Gawain and the Green Knight*, including those by M. R. Ridley, Gwyn Jones, and Brian Stone.

See also L. S. Brewer, *From Cuchulain to Gawain: Sourses and Analogues of Sir Gawain and the Green Knight*, Cambridge, 1973.

Chapter 8

SIR THOMAS MALORY: *Works* ed. Eugene Vinaver, Oxford, 1967.

Eugene Vinaver, *Malory*, Oxford, 1929.

William Matthews, *The Ill-framed Knight*, Cambridge and Los Angeles, 1966.

R. M. Lumiansky, ed., *Malory's Originality*, Baltimore, 1964.

Chapter 9

Sir Thomas Kendrick, *British Antiquity*, London, 1951.

R. F. Brinkley, *Arthurian Legend in the Seventeenth Century*, Baltimore, 1932.

M. W. MacCallum, *Tennyson's Idylls of the King and Arthurian Story from the XVIth Century*, Glasgow, 1894.

H. Maynadier, *The Arthur of the English Poets*, Cambridge, 1907.

M. J. C. Reid, *The Arthurian Legend: A Comparison of Treatment in Modern and Medieval Literature*, Edinburgh, 1937; rptd 1960.

N. C. Starr, *King Arthur Today*, Florida, 1954.

INDEX

(References to plates are in italics)

191